# PLYMOUTH AND TORQUAY TRAMWAYS

### Roy C Anderson

**Series editor Robert J Harley**

*Front cover photograph: Number 11 mounted on a Mountain and Gibson truck on arrival from Paignton stands outside the coach booking office in Vaughan Parade. The GWR commenced using this office in 1877 as a receiving office and also as the terminal of their bus service from Paignton which commenced on 11th July 1904 and ceased on 30th September 1911, following the trams running to Paignton. In 1913 the booking office was taken over by the South Devon Garage and Motor Touring Company which became part of Grey Cars in 1930. It was also the booking office for other operators including Royal Blue Automobile Services of Bournemouth which had originated as a horse drawn coach firm in 1880.*

*Back cover photograph upper: 151 is the experimental car designed by the General Manager Mr C.J.Jackson and built at Milehouse in 1925. Shown here in the original all teak livery, it lasted until 1945. The following production batch of cars were similar in appearance but incorporated many improvements arising from experience with this prototype.*

*Back cover photograph lower: In this view of the Cliff railway approach to the lower station at Oddicombe Beach we see the sand and blue sea for which Torbay is so famous. The Cliff railway has been a great attraction since it opened in 1926 to holiday makers and local residents.*

*Published July 2011*

*ISBN 978 1 906008 97 0*

*© Roy C Anderson, 2011*

*Design Deborah Esher*

*Published by*
    *Middleton Press*
    *Easebourne Lane*
    *Midhurst*
    *West Sussex*
    *GU29 9AZ*
*Tel: 01730 813169*
*Fax: 01730 812601*
*Email: info@middletonpress.co.uk*
*www.middletonpress.co.uk*

*Printed in the United Kingdom by Henry Ling Limited, at the Dorset Press, Dorchester, DT1 1HD*

# CONTENTS
*Picture numbers*

| | |
|---|---|
| Plymouth | 1 - 45 |
| Torquay | 46 - 119 |
| Babbacombe | 120 - 124 |

# INTRODUCTION AND ACKNOWLEDGEMENTS

My thanks go to Les Folkard in particular, together with Ken Brown and David Voice for their assistance with photographs and the manuscript; Roger Atkinson very kindly supplied images of the tickets. As well, I wish to acknowledge all those photographers who recorded the tramways in their operating days, without which our books would not be so informative. Sources of data are *A history of the Western National* written by myself and the late G.G.A.Frankis; *Devon General - a fascinating story* by Les Folkard; *Torbay Transport* by Fisher Barnham; *Tramways of the West of England* by P.W.Gentry; *Torquay Tramways* by R. Crawley; John Ayers of the Friends of the Babbacombe Cliff Railway; Torquay Tramways Company progress reports (1923);Torquay Tramways Co.Ltd rule book 1911; Torquay Corporation minutes; Torquay Corporation Abstract of accounts 1934/35; Paignton District Council minutes; *Plymouth 100 years of Street Transport* by the late R.C.Sambourne, whose researches have been so valuable in regard to the history of public transport in the South West of England. Maps are by the late John Gillham.

# GEOGRAPHICAL SETTING

Plymouth and Torquay are situated in South Devon. Plymouth is approximately thirty miles to the south west of Torquay and is a large city which is home to a Royal Navy base. Torquay is about twenty five miles south west of Exeter and is a major seaside holiday resort.

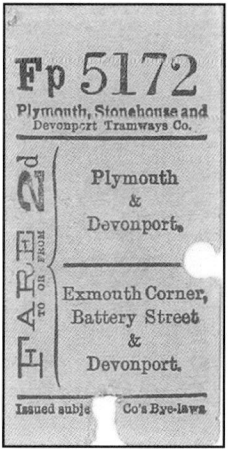
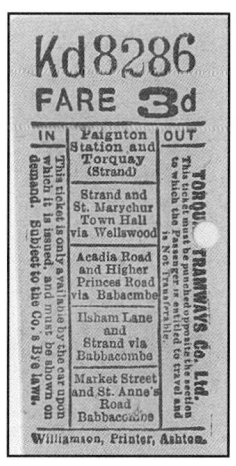

# 1. PLYMOUTH

*During the Second World War, the City of Plymouth was badly blitzed and after the war the city centre rebuilt. Please note that some of the roads referred to in this book may no longer exist but are shown on the map of the City which refers to pre 1939. Plymouth has the distinction of being the last street tramway in the south west of England but since its closure a narrow gauge tourist tramway on a private right of way was opened in 1969 at Seaton in Devon and continues to go from "strength to strength".*

## HISTORICAL BACKGROUND

Public passenger transport, using horse drawn buses, had been operating in Plymouth, Devonport, and Stonehouse since 1832 and several firms were involved in the business and did not welcome the establishment of tramways in the area of Plymouth, Devonport and East Stonehouse but in due course these towns were served by three tramway undertakings, and it was quite a complex situation. The first to commence operating was the Plymouth, Stonehouse and Devonport Tramways Co Ltd. Not only was it formed under the 1870 Tramways Act, but it was the first system to receive powers to construct a tramway system under this Act. With track laid to the standard gauge of 4ft 8½ inches (1435mm) in due course it served the two separate boroughs of Plymouth, Devonport and the urban district of Stonehouse, where a depot and stables were built. Worked with horse trams, the first line to be opened on 17th March 1872 was a trial service and no fares were charged; the service proper between Plymouth (Clock Tower) and Devonport (Cumberland gardens) commenced on the following day traversing a well populated dockside district. Also, in 1872, the company had become a subsidiary of the Provincial Tramways Company Limited. From the outset the companies tracks were laid on Stonehouse Bridge where there was a ½d toll to be paid later for each time a car crossed the bridge. In 1874 an extension was authorised into Devonport (Fore Street), inwards along Chapel Street and outwards via Albyn Street. Rolling stock was housed in a shed with adjoining stables in Manor Lane, Stonehouse and consisted of eight cars and seventy-six horses, two of which were required to draw each car and three extra to draw the car up Devonport Hill, which had a gradient of 1 in 11. By 1895 the company operated twelve open top double deck cars with outside transverse seats, whereas the original cars had knife board seating outside and were of smaller seating capacity.

In 1901 the track in Plymouth and Stonehouse was sold to the respective boroughs with the Company retaining the track in Stonehouse, between Edgecombe Street and Manor Street, all relaid to the narrower gauge of 3 feet 6 inches (1067mm) and the electrified system came into operation on 18th November 1901. For operating in Plymouth, where the overhead line was to the standard Plymouth Corporation design, the Corporation supplied the current from its own generating station at Prince Rock, but elsewhere current was supplied from the Devonport Corporation facility in Newport Street, Stonehouse. A new six road depot to house eighteen electric trams was built at the corner of Market Street and Edgemont Street in Stonehouse. A traverser was used to give access to roads 4 to 6. When in 1914 Plymouth Corporation extended its municipal boundary to include Devonport and Stonehouse, the company elected to continue working its single route from Plymouth to Stonehouse until its lease expired in 1922 and Plymouth Corporation purchased the undertaking. Originally, single track with passing places, it was later doubled except in Stonehouse where the track was single with loops.

Plymouth Corporation became actively involved as a tramway operator when it acquired The Plymouth, Devonport and District Tramways Company Limited, which had originated as a horse and steam undertaking and was granted powers in the early 1880s to construct and operate tramways in both Plymouth and Devonport, using mechanical traction. Five Wilkinson vertical boilered steam engines were acquired in 1884/5 and limited services commenced to Mannamead, Millbay, and North Road. There were numerous complaints of excessive noise, black smoke and obnoxious fumes from the steam locomotives, and bad time keeping. Finally the company gave up and in its place a company named the Plymouth Tramways Company took over working the services in 1889, drawing the cars with horses. The company proceeded with constructing tramways in Plymouth but did not do likewise in Devonport, with the result this local authority took the matter to Court and secured an injunction which prohibited the company from operating in Plymouth until it had constructed tramways in Devonport. Due to the lack of the necessary capital the company collapsed and in 1892 Plymouth Corporation acquired the company's property for £12,500, (it is presumed all the steam engines were disposed of and it is known that two were purchased by a works at Sevenoaks in Kent, where they worked until 1922), following which it proceeded to construct the authorised tramways and so the Plymouth Corporation Tramways Department was formed. After carrying out the necessary works the Corporation commenced horse drawn services, the first of which was from Millbay to West Hoe on 11th March 1893; Mutley Plain to Compton Lane End (where the depot was located)on 3rd April 1893;and to Prince Rock on 10th December 1896. Using horse drawn open top double deck cars painted vermillion and white with Plymouth Corporation Tramways in gold lettering on the rocker panel and the Corporation's crest on the waist panel, these cars seated 12 passengers inside and 12 outside and were kept in depots at Compton Lane End and West Hoe Road. As services developed, the number of cars increased to 17 necessitating a stud of 127 horses.

In 1898 Plymouth Corporation obtained powers to electrify the horse tramways and construct additional routes. This work commenced at once and was undertaken by the Electric Construction Company.

On 22nd September 1899, suitably decorated cars 1-6 were used for the opening ceremony and proceeded in file from Prince Rock to the Theatre (which became service 5).The four other services introduced over the next five years were:

1	Theatre - Mutley - Compton on 4th April 1901
2	Theatre - Mutley - Peverell on 13th January 1905
3	West Hoe (later Theatre) - Drake Circus - North Road Station
	(Pennycomequick)
	on 21st September 1905
4	Theatre-Drake Circus-Beaumont Road on 2nd April 1902

There was no regular service to West Hoe, cars running to the Hoe when necessary as were extensions to other services.

At first services were indicated by roller blind destination indicators and coloured discs attached to the car dash. These were later replaced by discs giving the service number. Cars were not fitted with head lamps until after WWI. Experience indicated that some changes to services might be desirable but the basic framework remained (apart from services 3 and 5 which were terminated at Theatre) until at various intervals the system was expanded.

The Devonport and District Tramways Co Ltd (D&D), formed in 1901, was a subsidiary of the British Electric Traction Company and the third company in the area to which powers were granted to construct a 3 feet 6 inch gauge tramway in Devonport and Stonehouse, to be worked on the overhead electric system and which was opened on 26th June 1901. Current was drawn from the Devonport Corporation power station in Newport Street, Stonehouse. The tramways constructed were from Morice Square to Camel's Head (Saltash Road ); Fore Street to Pennycomequick (Stuart Road) via Paradise Road; Paradise Road to Milehouse Road via Paradise Road and South Keyham to Trafalgar Road also

Albert Road to Paradise Road, giving a route mileage of 4.75 miles (7.6km).

In 1900 Devonport Corporation was given powers to construct tramways from Camel's Head to St Budeaux and Saltash passage also from North Keyham to Tor Lane Peverell, but the Corporation decided not to work the lines and as these two disconnected tramways were to all intents and purposes extensions of the Devonport and District lines, it is perhaps not surprising that the Corporation handed them over to the Company under lease. Due to the construction of an embankment, the Camel's Head to St Budeaux tramway operated in isolation (the two railheads being connected by a short wooden bridge)until 1903. It was worked on a shuttle service basis by two cars numbered 22 and 24 which were housed in a corrugated iron shed at Camel's Head.
The services operated were as follows:

Fore Street - Tor Lane via Stoke
Fore Street - Stuart Road via Wilton Street
Morice Square - St Budeaux - Saltash passage via Keyham
Morice Square - Tor Lane via St Levan Road
South Keyham - Stuart Road via Tamar Terrace (extended when required to St Budeaux and Saltash Passage)

D&D owned thirty-three trams which were originally painted maroon and cream, lined out in gold with the BET magnet and wheel device displayed centrally on the rocker panel. At the time the company was acquired by the Corporation, the livery was being changed to green and cream. Regrettably the company trams were involved in two serious accidents, both at Tamar Terrace Hill leading down to Paradise Road. On 27th September 1902 a car proceeding to Stuart Road was derailed and in the subsequent crash one person was killed and nine others injured. On 27th November 1914 number 25, whilst operating on the same route, conveying dock yard employees, ran away, was derailed and in the subsequent collision with a wall one person was killed and several were injured, two of whom later died.

In October 1914 following the merger of Plymouth, Devonport, and Stonehouse Urban District into one Borough, the tracks owned by Devonport Corporation passed to Plymouth Corporation, who made a generous offer to the D&D Co which sold out to Plymouth Corporation on 2nd October 1915. In the following year a junction was laid in at Pennycomequick to connect the two systems and through services to Devonport commenced in October 1916. The construction of the new line along Alma Road to Milehouse was delayed by WW I and it was not until 1st June 1922 that it was brought into use, bringing about further through travel facilities. Although other works were authorised this was the last to be constructed.

The Tramways Department was now responsible for operating all the tramways in Plymouth, Devonport, and Stonehouse and whilst the renewed and altered track work enabled new and revised services to be introduced, the outcome was not entirely satisfactory. Following the purchase by the Corporation of the Plymouth, Stonehouse, and Devonport Tramway at the expiry of its lease on 1st January 1922, the Corporation, which had owned the track used by the Company since 1901, laid in the curves to join the former PS & D leased track into the Corporation system. This enabled two circular services (2/2A and 6/6A) to be introduced and worked by ex P S & D trams converted to single enders. A terminal spur was laid in Fore Street for football specials, at which point the tramways reached their maximum route length of 117 miles 46 chains (188km). The full list of services as operative from 1923 is set out on the opposite page:

Thank you for shopping at Amazon.co.uk!

**Invoice for**
Your order of 24 September, 2011
Order ID 026-1441699-7962741
Invoice number DLQJJVxTN
Invoice date 25 September, 2011

**Billing Address**
**Mrs Lorna Leach**
63 Flanders Mansions
Flanders Road, Chiswick
London W4 1NF
United Kingdom

| Qty. | Item | Our Price (excl. VAT) | VAT Rate | Total |
|---|---|---|---|---|
| 1 | **Plymouth & Torquay Tramways: Including Babbacombe Cliff Lift (Tramway Classics)**<br>Hardcover. 1906008973<br>(** P-1-F54D181 **) | £15.15 | 0% | £15.15 |
| | Shipping charges | | | £0.00 |
| | Subtotal (excl. VAT) 0% | | | £15.15 |
| | Total VAT | | | £0.00 |
| | Total | | | £15.15 |

Conversion rate - £1.00 : EUR 1,14

**This shipment completes your order.**

You can always check the status of your orders or change your account details from the "Your Account" link at the top of each page on our site.

**Thinking of returning an item? PLEASE USE OUR ON-LINE RETURNS SUPPORT CENTRE.**

Our Returns Support Centre (www.amazon.co.uk/returns-support) will guide you through our returns process and provide you with a printable personalised return label. Please have your order number ready (you can find it next to your order summary, above). Our Returns Policy does not affect your statutory rights.

Amazon EU S.a.r.L, 5 Rue Plaetis, L-2338, Luxembourg
VAT number : GB727255821
**Please note - this is not a returns address - for returns - please see above for details of our online returns centre**

45/DQQvJ2xTN/-1 of 1-///1M/econ-uk/5358915/0926-16:45/0926-08:14/turquhar Pack Type - A3

| | |
|---|---|
| 1 | Theatre - Sherwell - Hyde Park - Compton |
| 2 | Theatre - Hyde Park - Peverell - Milehouse - Fore Street - Theatre |
| 2A | Reverse of 2 |
| 3 | Theatre - Peverell - Milehouse - Ford Hill - North Keyham - Morice Square |
| 4 | Beaumont Road - St.Judes - Drake Circus - Theatre - Millbay |
| 5 | Prince Rock - Drake Circus - Theatre - Millbay |
| 6 | Theatre - Pennycomequick - Wilton Street - Fore Street - Stonehouse - Theatre |
| 6A | Theatre - Pennycomequick - Wilton Street - South Keyham - Wolseley Road - St.Budeaux |
| 7A | Theatre - South Keyham |
| 8 | Morice Square - North Keyham - St.Budeaux |
| 9 | Theatre - Peverell - Milehouse - Alma Road - Theatre (14 miles long in a circuit) |
| 9A | Reverse of 9 |
| 10 | Theatre - Pennycomequick - Milehouse - North Keyham - Morice Square |
| 11 | Beaumont Road - Theatre - Edgecome Street - Fore Street |
| 12 | Prince Rock - Theatre - Fore Street |
| 14 | Theatre - Alma Road - Milehouse - South Keyham - Wolseley Road - St Budeaux - Saltash Passage (the longest route of 9 miles) |
| 14A | Theatre - Milehouse - South Keyham |

To improve facilities further there was considerable doubling of tracks and the substitution of span wiring of the overhead rather than the use of bracket arms, although some remained to suit the particular circumstances. Appropriate automatic changing of points and the direction of the overhead was established at strategic locations and activated from the trolley, or manually by switches on the poles.

Services 9 and 9A were withdrawn in 1923, the replacement route cut back to Peverell and given a service letter P. The next tram service closure was the service from Morice Square to Saltash passage which took place on 27th October1930 and all main routes were closed by 9th May 1937 except for service 11, although trams were used in connection with the Bath and West show in Central Park from 25th to 28th May 1938. Some workmen's cars continued to work until 15th March 1939 although most of the four wheeled trams had been withdrawn by 1937. The tram fleet never exceeded 127 cars at any one time, despite numbered 1 to 166. During the programmed period of closure the former tram depots at Compton were closed and sold in 1933 and Prince Rock in May 1937 after which it was demolished.

Early in 1937 the remaining tram service numbers, 2 and 2A, were co-ordinated with those for the buses and became services 1 and 2 which were the final tramway closures on 9th May 1937 except for service P which was numbered 11. Extended from the Guildhall to Theatre it was the last tram service to operate in Plymouth, apart from some workmen's specials. At the outbreak of WW2, in September 1939, the service from Theatre to Peverell (route 11) was still in operation although closed for a month in March 1941, due to air raid damage to the track and overhead. When the service resumed it was only between Theatre and Old Town Street and it continued until 29th September 1945. Thus ended tramway operation in Plymouth and it was stated in the Mayor's speech, that over the years the trams had conveyed 800 million passengers and operated 70 million passengers, an average of eleven passengers for every mile run!

# ROLLING STOCK

By the end of 1915, the Plymouth Corporation fleet consisted of 55 cars and with the exception of six single deckers (37-42) all were four wheel open top cars. Numbers 1-6 were delivered in 1899 for the opening of the tramway and were built by Brush, uncanopied and mounted on Peckham cantilever trucks with Westinghouse equipment and seating forty two passengers. Fourteen similar cars, but with a veranda balcony, also built by Brush with Peckham cantilever trucks and numbered 7-20, were delivered in 1900. At a later date number 12 received a Brill 21E truck believed to have come from a former Devonport and District car. In 1903 there was a change of builder when Milnes supplied ten balcony cars numbered 21-30. Numbers 21-26 were mounted on Cantilever trucks and 27-30 were on Brush Conalty trucks. Another six Brush built balcony cars numbered 31-36 were delivered in 1905 to be followed in 1906 by six small single deckers numbered 37-42, built by Brush on Brill 21E 5ft 6inch wheelbase trucks. These cars were constructed for one man operation on the West Hoe to North Road railway station service. Brush also built the next batch of twelve balcony cars numbered 43-54 in 1915 and in due course all these cars received slipper brakes and half turn stairs where not so supplied at time of build. The 55th car was an unnumbered open sided rail grinder.

Thirty-three cars were taken over by Plymouth Corporation in 1915 with the acquisition of the D&D. Fifteen were renumbered 55-69 immediately (and renumbered again when the new Brush cars were delivered to the Corporation in 1916 and 17) and seven were scrapped at time of take over. Subsequently further ex D&D cars were brought into the Corporation fleet and the retained twenty six, many of which were rebuilt in the Milehouse workshops receiving canopies and normal stairs where necessary, were numbered 63-88 (including those renumbered for a second time).

In 1916 and 17 Brush built canopied cars for the Corporation, mounted on Peckham P22 trucks numbered 55 to 58 and 60/61 (taking numbers of already renumbered ex D&D cars which had to be changed again!). These were followed in 1918 by 90 and 92 which are believed to be the missing 59 and 62 from the original batch of eight. There was no number 89; 91 and 93 were rebuilt at Milehouse from ex D&D stock on Brill 21E trucks. Numbers 108-111 were left blank and 112 was a canopied car with normal stairs built in the workshops at Milehouse. A further 12 canopied cars built by Brush on Peckham P22 trucks and with normal stairs, numbered 94-105, came in 1919/20 (this order had been reduced by two which were supplied to Exeter and were later sold to Plymouth). At the same time the Corporation built several cars at the Milehouse workshops similar to 55-62 and numbered 91, 93 and 112 incorporating parts from ex D&D cars and mounted on Brill 21E trucks. Plymouth Corporation trams were not fitted with headlamps until after WWI and the work of installation was then undertaken in the Milehouse workshops.

The acquisition of the PS&D Tramways Co in 1922 brought another fifteen cars (renumbered 113-127) into the Corporation fleet. Of these 114-123 were rebuilt as single enders for use on circular routes 2/2A and 6/6A The front end was restructured and the cars only had one set of stairs at the rear. At the same time 124-127 were rebuilt, in conventional style, and converted 119 was again rebuilt to bring it into line with these cars. Number 113 was not altered. In 1922 five of the six "demi cars" which had been used on services to the Hoe and Piers were scrapped but number 42 was retained and became a works car. Until 1922 the livery was bright red and cream but a new livery of primrose and cream was introduced, but this did not prove satisfactory. Whereas new trams and buses were being turned out in a livery of teak lined out in gold this also did not find favour and was changed to a drab speckled brown livery. This also proved impractical and when a new transport manager was appointed in 1929, he introduced a new livery for buses and trams of maroon and cream which was applied to all the tram fleet in eighteen months.

In 1924 twenty new four wheel open top cars were built by the English Electric Co Ltd (formerly the Dick Kerr Company), on Brill 21E 7ft 6inch wheelbase trucks and numbered 131-150 were delivered. With angular dashes and vestibules they became known to the staff as "Square Faces". All cars were equipped with roller blind destination indicator boxes and a similar box for displaying the route number. However, in 1924 coloured destination boards were fitted to some cars on the side waist rail and on the dash above the fleet number. Could this have been to promote new routes following the final merger in 1922?

Due to the long waiting times in the mid 1920s for the building of new trams by the remaining manufacturers the recently appointed transport manager was authorised to construct trams in the workshops at

Milehouse. He designed a high capacity open top bogie car numbered 151, for which the body was constructed in solid teak and fitted with plush seats on both decks. Besides building the body the Milehouse workshops built the maximum traction bogies. The only outside item was the electric equipment supplied by the English Electric Company. During testing the only real problem was that on certain curves the rear pony wheels derailed, but the problem was thought to have been solved by strengthening the check rails. Further, similar cars were built numbered 152 - 166. The final one to enter service was 166 in March 1928 but the problem with the trucks had not been solved and between 1930 and 1935 the bogie trucks of cars in this batch (except 156, 163, and 164 which retained their bogie trucks and were scrapped in 1942) had their bogie trucks replaced with a single long four wheel truck.

Also the Department took the opportunity to purchase a number of second hand trams to enable it to scrap a number of the older worn out cars in 1931, following the purchase, in that year, of nine four wheel open top vestibuled cars from Exeter Corporation whose tramways had closed. Plymouth given numbers 1-5 & 7 were on Brill 21E trucks and the remainder (6, 8, and 9) on Peckham P22 trucks. All had Brush bodies. Interestingly, former Exeter, now Plymouth, 8 and 9 were originally ordered for Plymouth in 1920 but upon cancellation of this order these cars were supplied to Exeter.

In 1933, consequent upon the forthcoming closure of the Torquay tramway system in 1934, Plymouth Corporation purchased six four wheel unvestibuled open top cars built by Brush on Brill 21E trucks, which were all scrapped in 1936. Also purchased were six open top vestibuled cars built by Brush and mounted on Brush 3L maximum traction bogie trucks. All these cars were scrapped in 1942. They had the reputation of being superb riders, but drivers had to be careful on some curves not to attempt to pass another car proceeding in the opposite direction. Perhaps the Tramways Department might have been served better if they had fitted this type of truck to their own build cars rather than manufacturing their own bogie trucks.

*Note that Plymouth, Stonehouse and Devonport cars are referred to as PS&D, Devonport and District as D&D, Plymouth Devonport and District Tramway as PDDT and Plymouth Corporation as PCT.*

Plymouth 1914

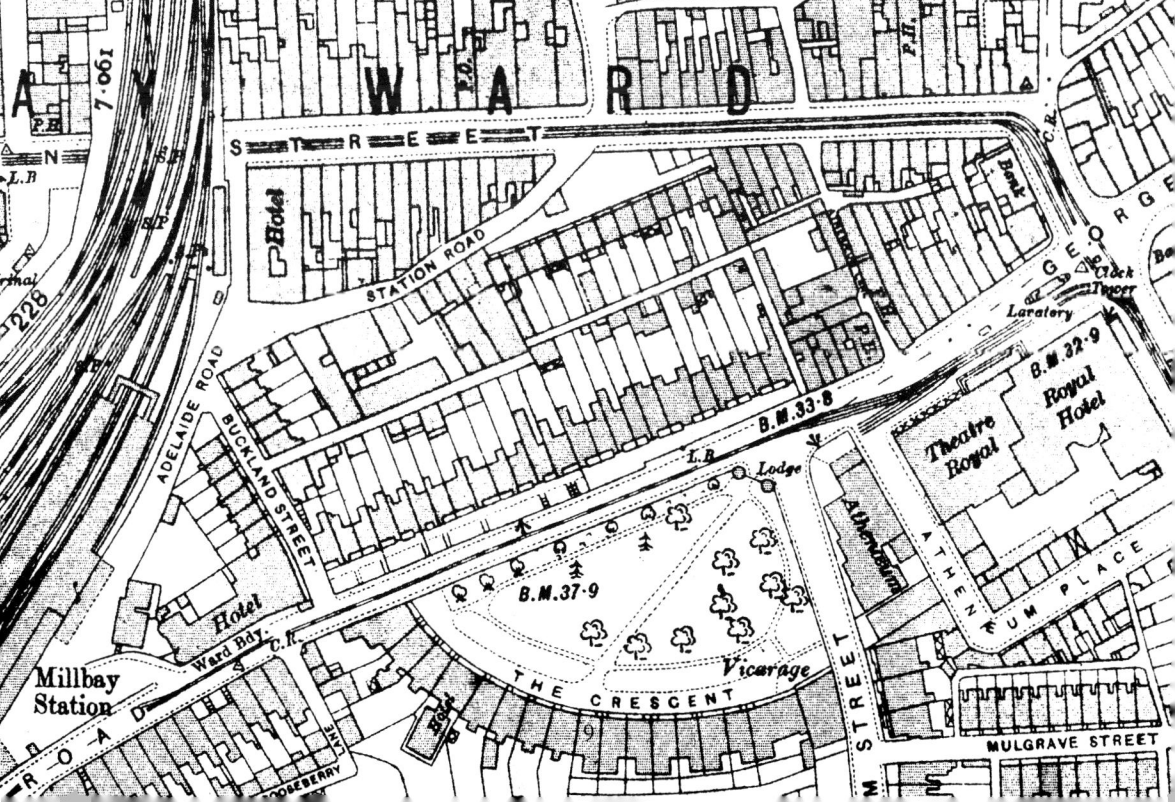

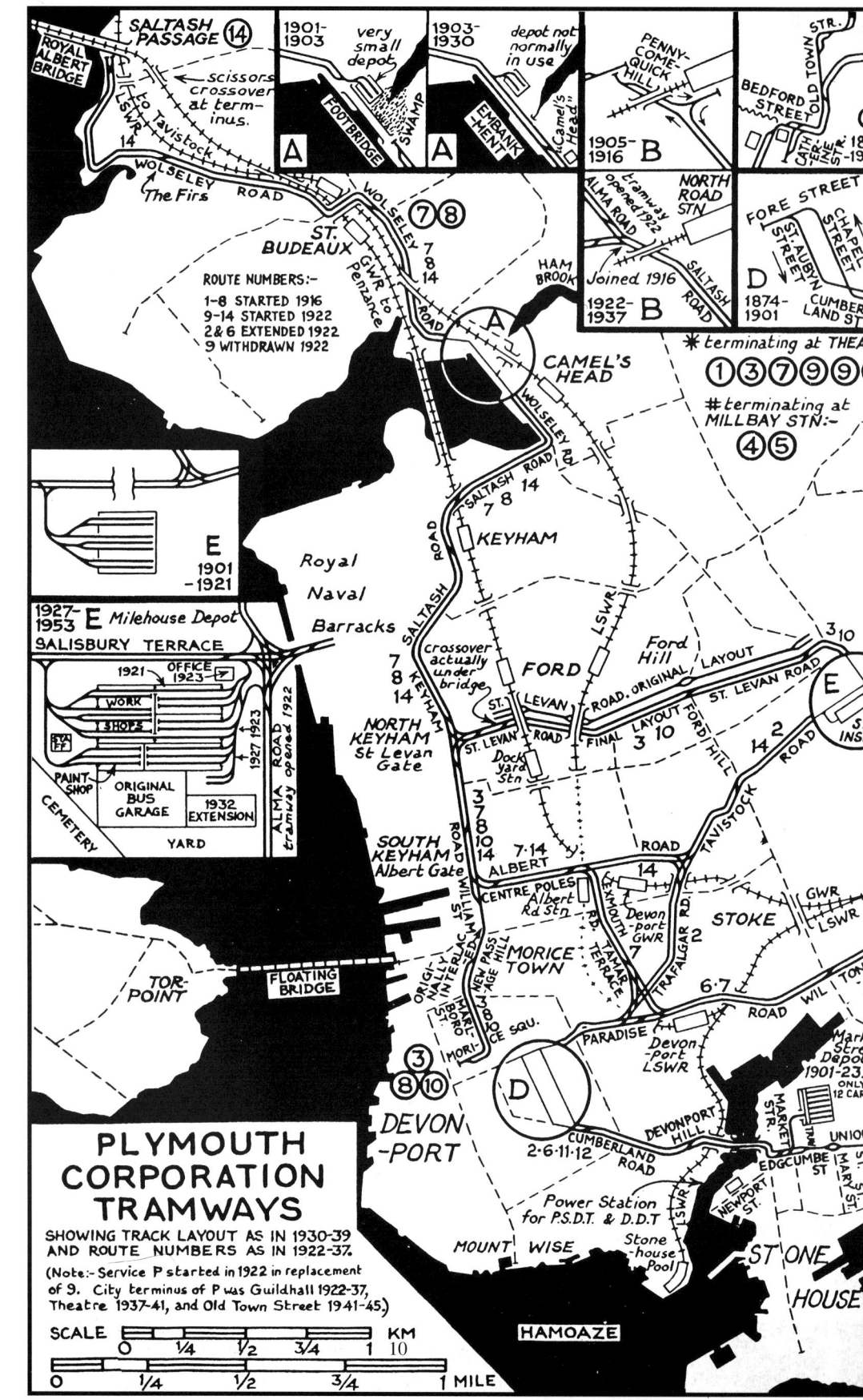

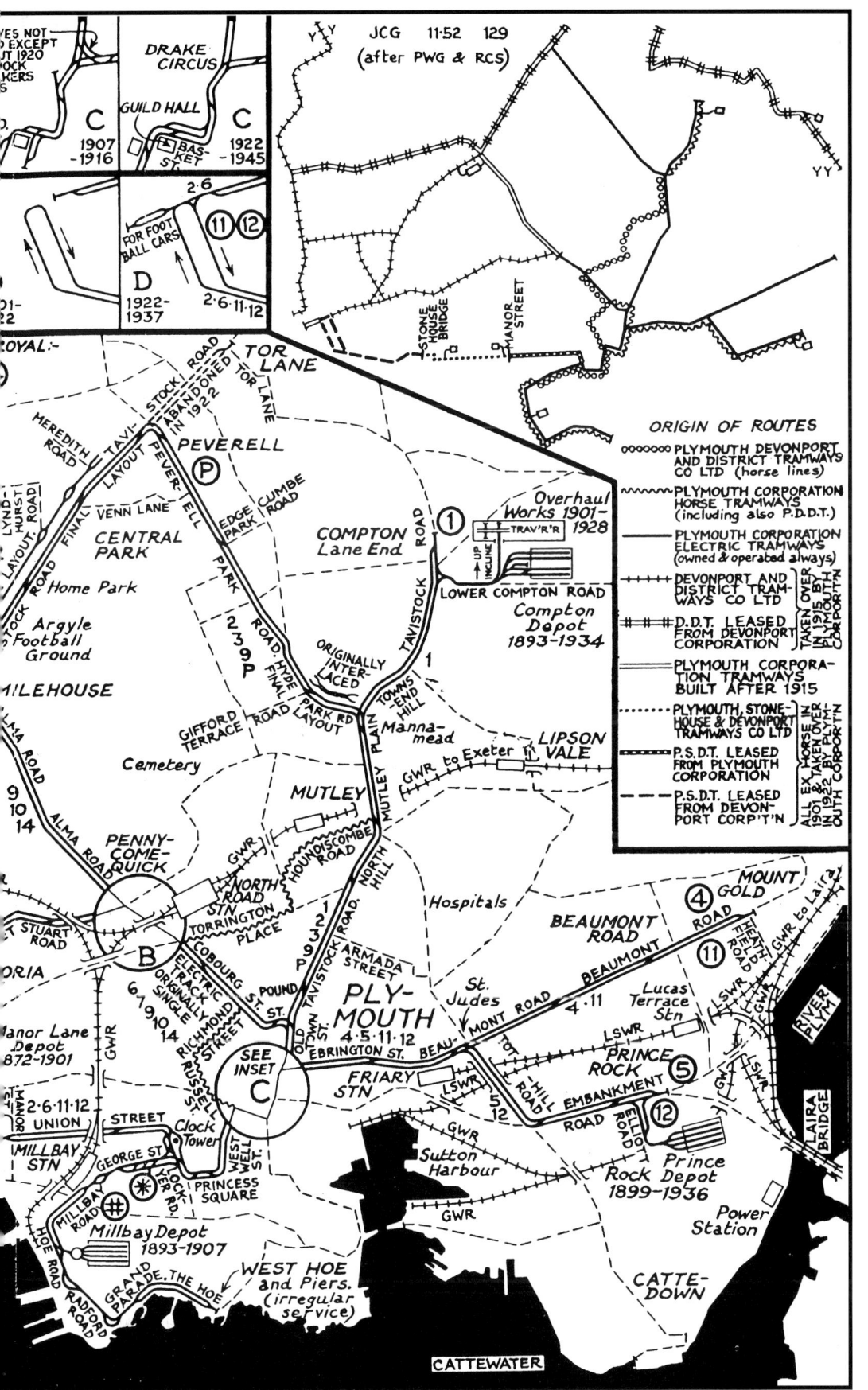

1. Entering the loop at the Octagon in 1902 is a PS&D horse drawn tram.
Note that the two driving horses are in perfect step.

2. The horse tram tracks lead away at the left to Millbay railway station and the Hoe and piers in this photograph taken in George Street in 1895.

3. Also in 1895 three trace horses have been attached to this PS&D horse tram to assist in the climb up Devonport Hill.

4. Circa 1900 this PS&D tram drawn by two horses is entering Billing Street loop outside the Grand Theatre in Union Street.

5. On route from Compton lane End to Market Place a well loaded PCT car passes through the then tree lined Mutley Plain.

6. Ending its days in 1922 at Swanscombe Colliery Kent is one of the five steam locomotives used by the PDDT.

7. PS&D car number 11 stands at the terminus in Fore Street Devonport prior to departing for Plymouth.

8. D&D number 21 is at St Budeaux. This car has the repositioned headlamp and advertisements on the stair risers.

9. PS&D car is on the ½ penny toll bridge at Stonehouse in 1910.

10. Standing at Prince Rock is PCT number 24 from the second batch of cars numbered 21 to 30 supplied by Milnes on Peckham trucks in 1903. Like previous cars they had no headlamps.

11.    Circa 1910, one of the original D&D trams on route from Morice Square to St Budeaux passes the gate to the St.Levan Royal Naval dockyard.

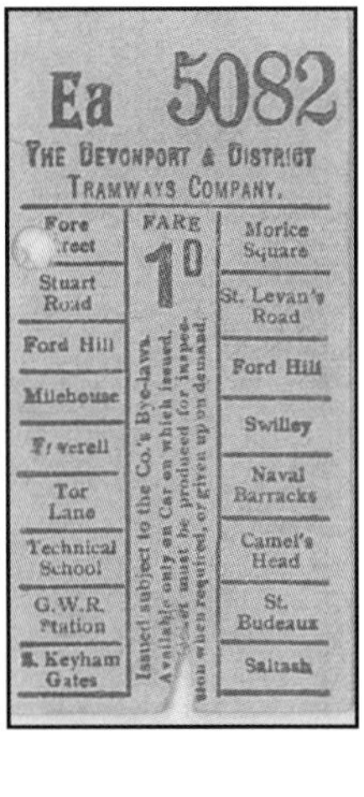

12. On 27th November 1914 D&D car number 25 crashed into the wall of the LSWR station after running out of control down the steep terrace. One man was killed and several injured. This was the second fatal accident on this section of track.

13. PCT trams 18 and 19 are traversing Mutley Plain on the Compton and Peverall routes.

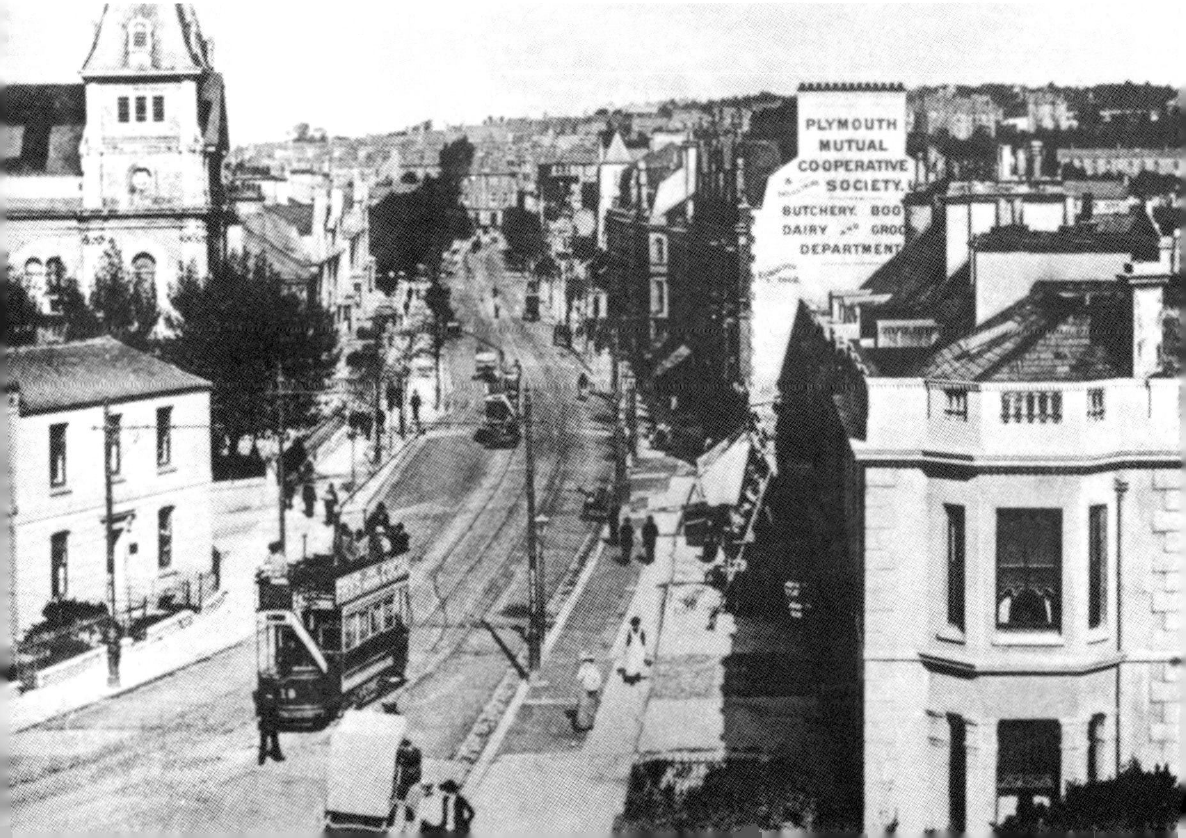

14. In 1914 PS&D tram number 9 was at St Andrews Cross prior to entering Basket Street.

**Stations around Plymouth can also be found in**
*Branch Lines around Plymouth,*
*Tavistock to Plymouth,*
*Branch Lines to Launceston & Princetown,*
*Newton Abbot to Plymouth,*
*Plymouth to St. Austell* **and**
*Brunel - a railtour of his achievements.*

15. Common users; PS&D tram follows a PCT tram along Union Street.

16. One of the original PCT trams showing a red indicator stands at Cattedown Corner on route from Prince Rock to Theatre.

17. PCT 29 is at Theatre terminus.

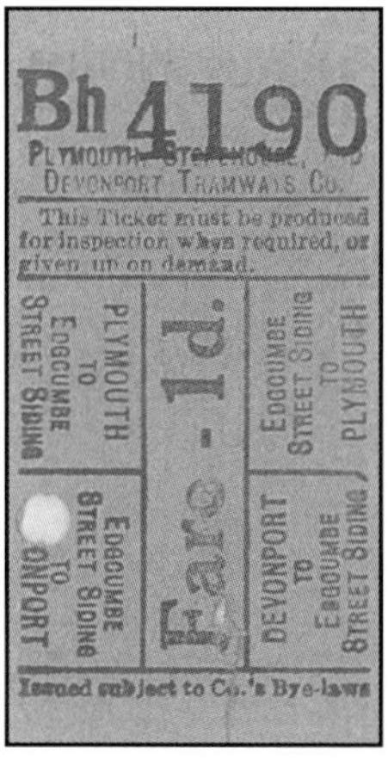

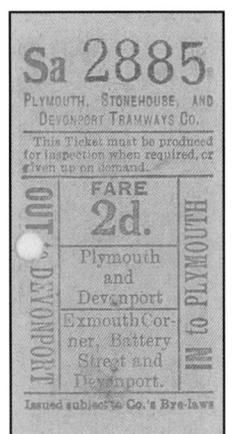 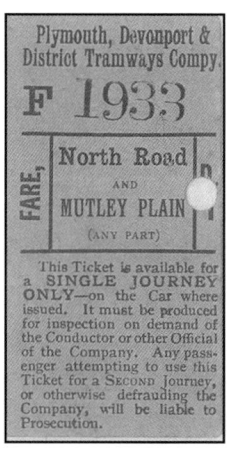

18. In 1921 original PCT car number 2 as rebuilt stands at Prince Rock prior to departing on service 9 to Theatre.

19. In 1920 an original D&D car of the 1-20 batch and numbered 80 in the PCT fleet turns from Old Town Street at St Andrews Cross.

20. Built at the Milehouse depot, no. 112 is being demonstrated to the Plymouth Corporation. Tramways Committee. Mr H.P Stokes the PCT General Manager is on the platform and wearing a boater hat.

➔ 21. Number 74 is one of three ex D &D cars (the others numbered 79 and 83) rebuilt in Milehouse depot with extended canopies and painted in the primrose livery.

22. Buses and trams were both maintained in Milehouse depot and in this photograph we see a Straker Squire bus and several trams including number 42 which is over the pit.

23. This line up of trams in Milehouse depot includes a Guy bus numbered 18.

24. Maintenance vehicles in the yard at Milehouse include on the left the lorry mounted tower wagon and the welding car built from ex demi car number 42.

25. This unnumbered rail grinder generally worked at night so was not often seen. Regrettably on one occasion it ran out of control crashing into the Plymouth Co-op Chambers and tragically killing the driver.

26. A former D&D car was used as a works car along with 33 and 75. All three were stripped out for this purpose.

27. Cars with the squared off dashes were nicknamed "Squarefaces" by the staff. Car 137 was one of a batch of 20 built by English Electric on Brill 21E trucks. Delivered in 1924 this car was withdrawn in 1938.

28. Number 98, repainted in the maroon and cream livery, was photographed in Chapel Street, Devonport whilst working a "special".

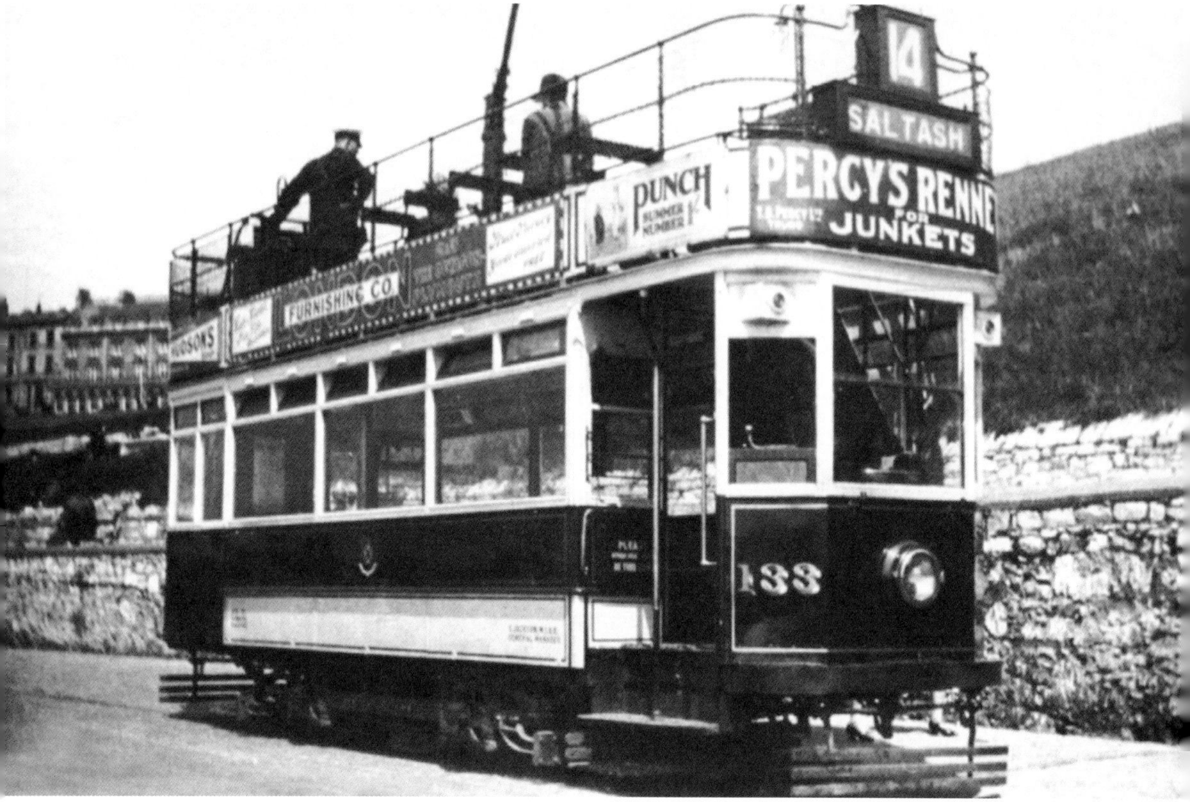

29. Another car of the batch delivered in 1924 number 133 is in the maroon and cream livery and was photographed in August 1930 working on the tramways longest route to Saltash Passage. Although "Saltash" is shown on the destination indicator no tram ever crossed the river Tamar into Cornwall.

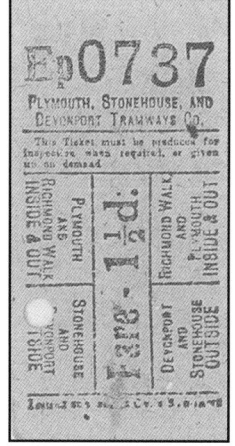

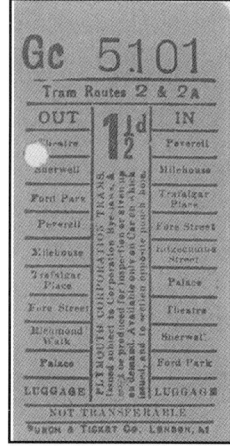

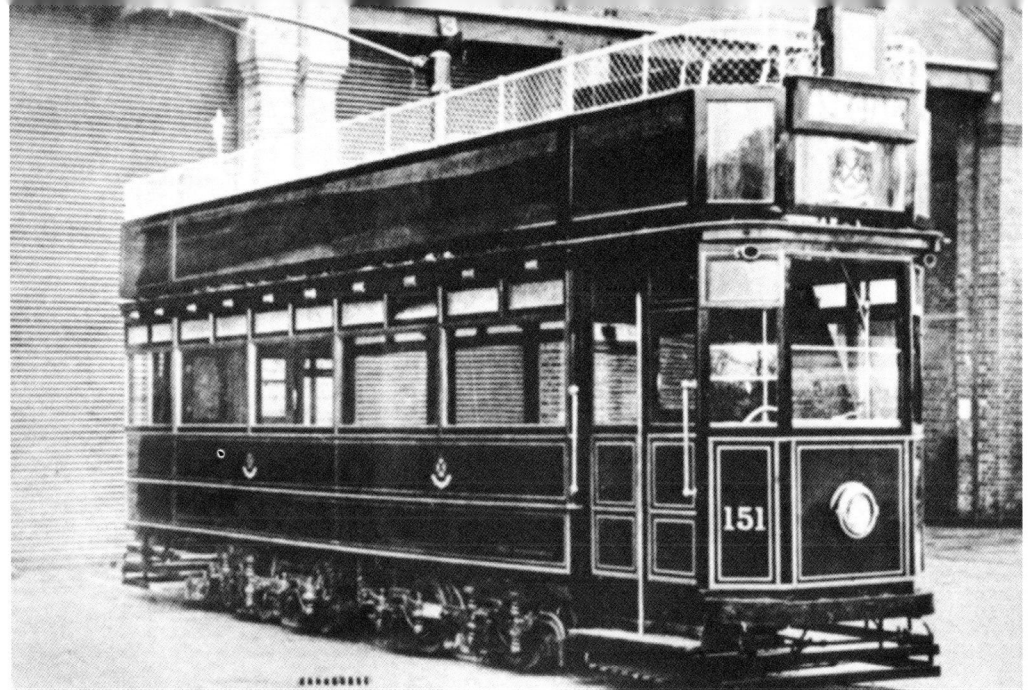

30. No. 151 is the experimental car designed by the General Manager Mr C.J.Jackson and built at Milehouse in 1925. Shown here in the original all teak livery it lasted until 1945. The following production batch of cars were similar in appearance but incorporated many improvements arising from experience with this prototype.

31. One of the experimental trucks for 151 and 15 similar cars. These bogie trucks were not entirely satisfactory and on all but three of these cars they were replaced with a long wheelbase four wheel truck. Perhaps it might have been better to have used a tried and tested bogie truck produced by an established manufacturer.

32. Top deck of 151 shows leather covered seats.

33. Upholstered longitudinal seating is depicted in the interior of car 151.

34. Number 164 is at Fore Street Devonport in 1936 still with its bogie trucks. Note the white summer hat covers worn by the crew.

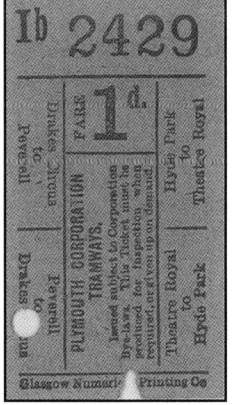
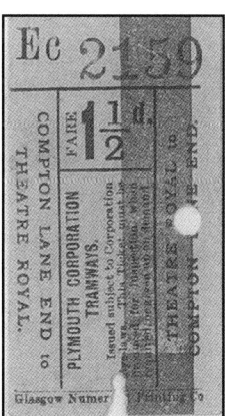

35. Former Exeter car was numbered 1 in the PCT fleet.

36. Former Torquay car fitted with Brush bogies was working in Plymouth in 1934 and was numbered 11. These cars had the largest seating capacity in the PCT fleet.

37. The pier which was destroyed in the Blitz of 1941 has its entrance from the Hoe which is where car 9 is standing.

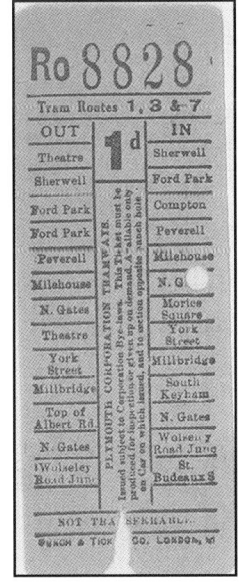 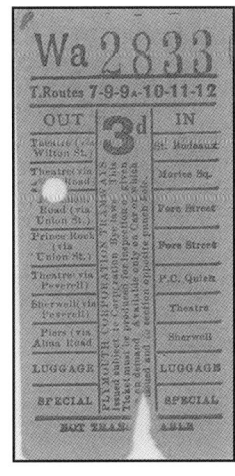

38. Former Exeter car 6 is seen with PCT cars in Milehouse depot.

39. Here we see three cars at Theatre. On the left one two former Exeter cars, and on the right a former PS&D car much rebuilt for single ended operation on the circular service.

40. Also at the central terminal is car 147 built by English Electric in 1924. It has vestibuled platforms and normal stairs and was scrapped in 1938.

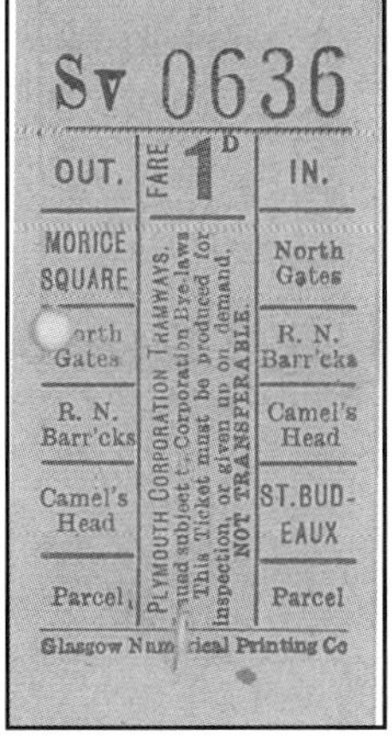

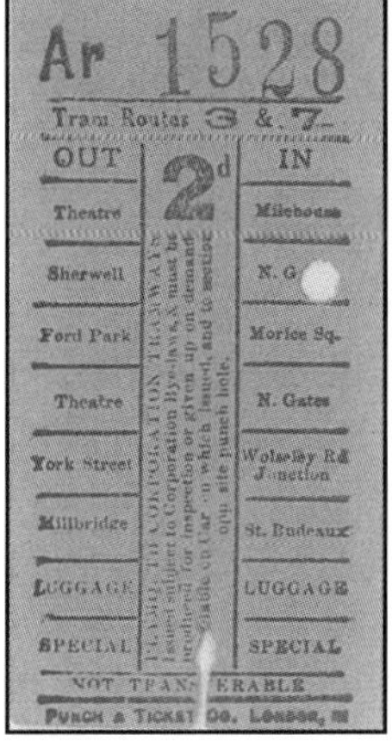

41. Number 151 in service is still in all teak livery. Note the opening windows for ventilation not carried forward on cars in the production batch. Similarly the destination indicator is positioned on the top deck rails whereas on the other fifteen the indicator is fitted to the platform canopy.

42. Fitted with a four wheel truck in place of bogies no. 158 passes through the blitzed central area of Plymouth. This car sustained wartime damage but was repaired and became Plymouth's last tram on 2nd August 1945.

43. This views shows a postwar reconstruction of Drake Circus. In front of the old building can be seen the tracks and crossover at the former terminal in Plymouth of of the P S &D tramway.

44. D&D car no. 4 was one of the original batch, numbered 1-20, built in the USA by the J.G.Brill Car Co and was supplied for the opening of the tramway. The livery then was chocolate and cream which was being changed to green and cream when the undertaking was acquired by Plymouth Corporation.

45. No. 37 was the first of the five demi cars built for "one man operation" by Brush in 1906. They were scrapped in 1924, except for no. 42 which was converted to a welding car and lasted until 1945.

# 2. TORQUAY
# HISTORICAL BACKGROUND

In the 19th century, the town of Torquay grew from a fishing village to become a fashionable holiday resort. In 1848 the railway arrived at Torre Station accompanied by the development of hotels and residential areas including the erection of many fine houses and new and improved roads. Public passenger transport originating in 1842 consisted of horse drawn buses and cabs and on 24th June 1872 a regular horse drawn bus service commenced between Torquay and Paignton, then two separate local authority areas.

In 1903 the Dolter Electric Traction Company Limited offered to lay a system of tramways (using the surface contact system) in Torquay "free of all costs to the ratepayer" on condition the Council would provide the current for which the Company would become a customer. A French invention, the Dolter system dispensed with overhead wiring and poles and was a surface contact system by which the tram drew current from plates between the rails fed by a continuous electrical cable also buried in the roadway between the rails. The necessary powers were granted in a Tramways Order dated August 1904 allowing lines to be laid from Strand-Torre Station-Market Street-Ellacombe-St.Marychurch Road-Brunswick Square-Babbacombe-Strand The British Thompson Houston Company Limited supplied the electrical equipment and track laying commenced at Torre station on 23rd October 1905 to a gauge of 3 feet 6 inches (1067mm). Insofar as the work required installation of the Dolter surface contact system this took considerably more time than for a straight forward overhead wired system, but it met the objection of Torquay residents who opposed the erection of overhead wires and their supporting structures.

The track was single with loops but some were quite long in particular that running down from Torwood Street through the Strand to Fleet Street, also at Ellacombe. There was a short length of single track in front of the Grand Hotel which was doubled in 1926 and joined to the Paignton section which was double track from its inception. When the bogie cars were delivered it was necessary to re lay the track in Vaughan Parade to ease the curve. All points were single tongued and were operated by the motorman with a bar. The only exception was the junction between Market Street and Union Street where a point's man was employed, and spring points for the passing loop near the Palace Hotel. Electric light signals were originally installed on the single and loop sections between Forest Road and Hatfield Road, Ellacombe but these were later disused and automatic semaphore signals were provided to protect the single line in Hatfield Road only. On the St Marychurch –Wellswood section the single line immediately north of St Matthias Church was protected. When the overhead conversion was made switches for the signal lights were incorporated in the wiring and activated by the trolleys. A similar arrangement was built in to operate some points.

The official opening took place on 4th April 1907 and for the opening ceremony three undecorated cars numbered 18, 4, and 13 were lined up in Victoria parade at Beacon Quay. Only 18 and 4 were use to convey the official party which included the mayor, Councillors, and Officials and invited guests. The cars moved off to Torre Station with the Mayor at the controls (supervised by motorman Charles Pugh) and returned via St Marychurch and Ellacombe. After the inaugural run the officials and guests retired to the Bath rooms for the inaugural lunch. Number 13 had not been required and there was little enthusiastic demonstration from the relatively small crowd attending but in the next five days after the opening 23,400 passengers rode on the trams and the weekly average settled down to an 40,000/50,000 passengers with this increasing to 100,000 during Regatta week.

The first three routes which commenced after the opening consisted of one from Beacon Quay to Torre station via Union Street; a second from Brunswick Square to St Marychurch via Upton; and the third from St Marychurch to Union Street via Ellacombe.The opening of the remaining tramway from the Strand to St Marychurch via Wellswood and Babbacombe was delayed until

11th November 1907 as the road at Torwood Mount had to be widened. The opening of this section enabled the circular service to be introduced. It should be noted that there were several sections on these routes that had sharp curves and steep inclines.

Torquay railway station adjacent to the Grand Hotel opened on the 2nd August 1859 and on 7th January 1908 powers had been granted for the laying of a tramway using the Dolter surface pick up system from Vaughan parade along Torbay Road to the Grand Hotel. Construction commenced on 11th February 1908 and the Board of Trade gave permission for the new tramway to be opened without a formal inspection which was undertaken at a later date. It was the last piece of surface contact tramway to be opened in Great Britain. A trial run was undertaken on 12th April 1908 and the tramway opened on 16th April 1908 when the Mayor drove decorated number 15 from Vaughan Parade to the Grand Hotel. There was more ceremony this time and number 15 remained in service on opening day fully decorated.

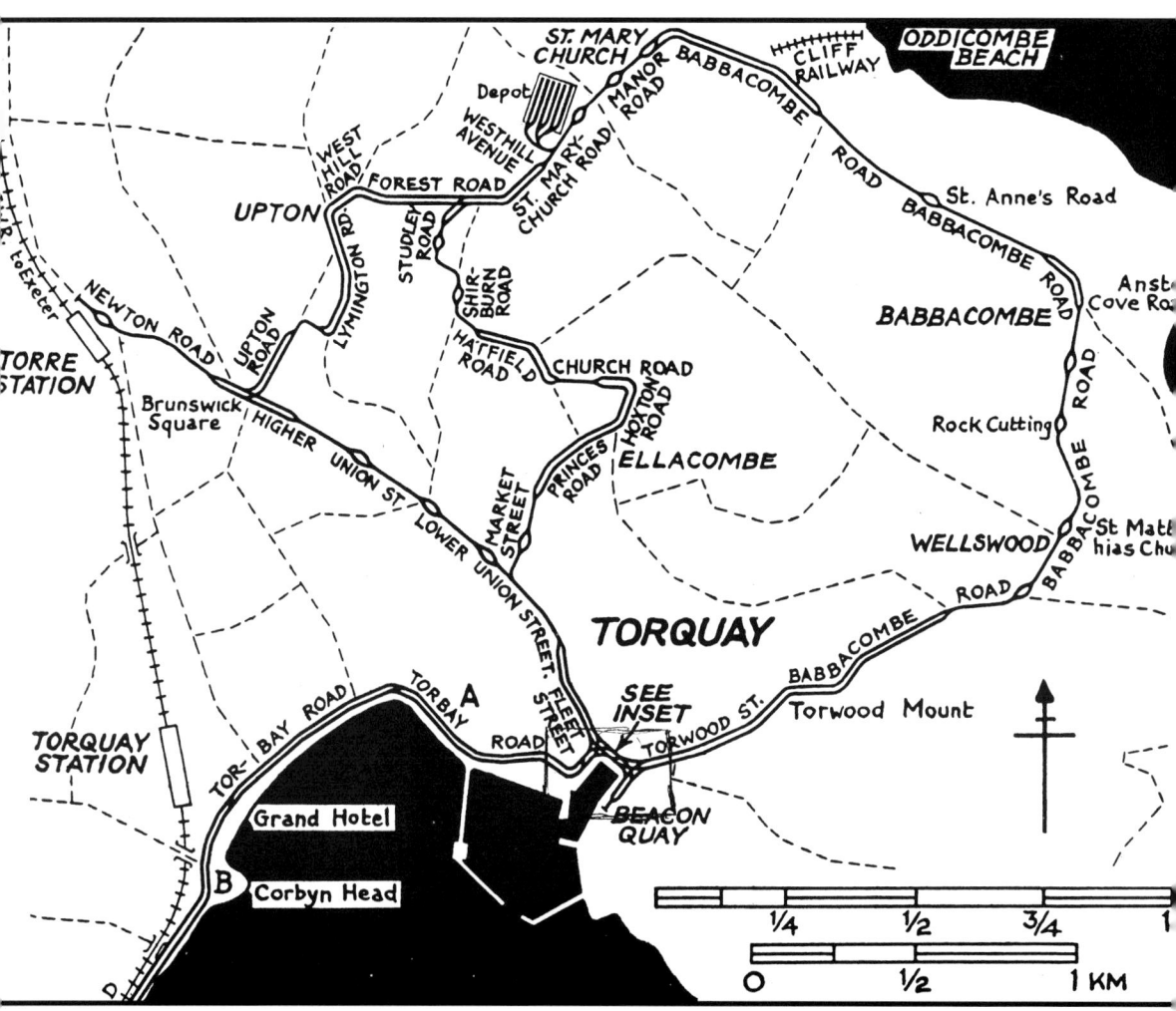

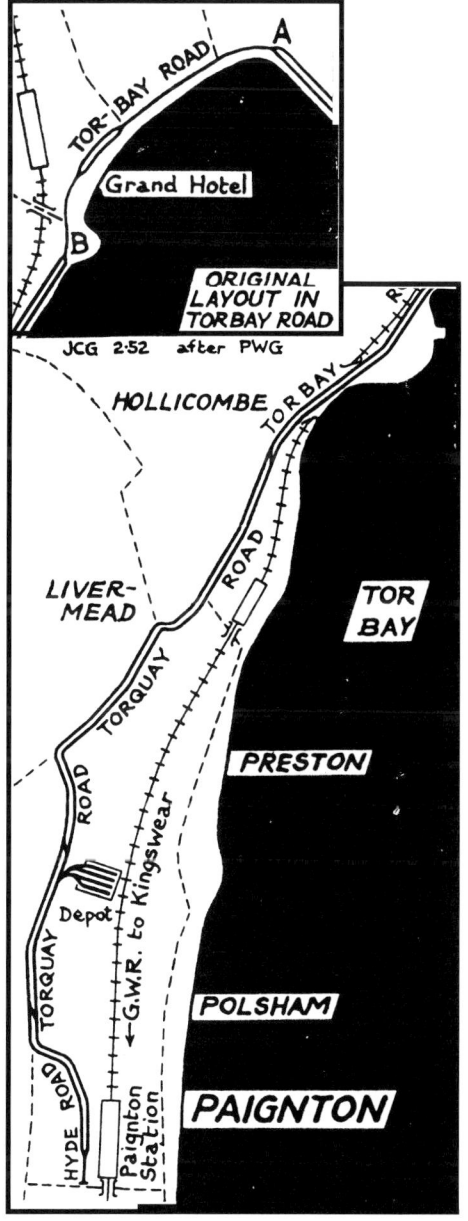

# THE DOLTER SYSTEM

This extraordinary and now wholly extinct method of propulsion can best be described as electrical leap frog. Providing current at 550 volts DC by means of an electrical cable which was laid beneath the road surface centrally between the rail tracks and was connected at regular intervals with the Dolter box made from an insulated ceramic material. Underneath the tram two skates were suspended polarised north and south energised from the car's operating current or from a bank of batteries installed within the tram which activated the first contact plate and then cut out .With the car moving the car passed over a Dolter surface box and the two metal plates were magnetised which attracted a pivotal arm inside the ceramic box. Upon rising, this closed a set of contacts and the current flowed through the plate via the skates to the cars controller and thence into the motors .When the car had passed, the magnetic field ceased, cutting off the supply of current and the road surface plate became inert. Trams tended to get struck between plates! This was due to a plate being dead and the one behind remaining live after the car had passed over it. A smaller skate followed the two main skates and if it passed over a plate which had remained live caused a bell to ring on the car and warn the crew. When this happened the conductor had to stop the car and alight in order to nail a piece of insulation material over the offending plate. All this with 550 volts DC! With this type of defect occurring more frequently a gang of men were employed for this purpose and "nick named" the "Dolter murderers!" The Dolter system proved costly and wasteful of current, besides a danger to other traffic, not to mention the hazards to human and animal life. The following description of a journey on a tram powered by this method (not a Torquay tram in this instance) makes hair raising reading;-

"As we passed over connectional plates, we seemed at times to be travelling over sheets of fire, the electric flashes and anon blazing from beneath the wheels with startling vividness ,caused I believe by skidding over the plates and not finding contact evenly. With the flash there came a swishing sound similar to sending off a burning rocket. The lights in the car too, danced in and out with a frivolous frequency. Altogether the effect on a night journey lent a spice of variety to a run".

Trams manoeuvring in the depot in Westhill Avenue did so by plugging in a cable attached to the tram into a wall mounted plug.

---

**A full description of the Dolter system is given in the companion Middleton Press volume *Hastings Tramways*.**

**Railway stations in the Torquay area can be found in *Branch Line to Kingswear*.**

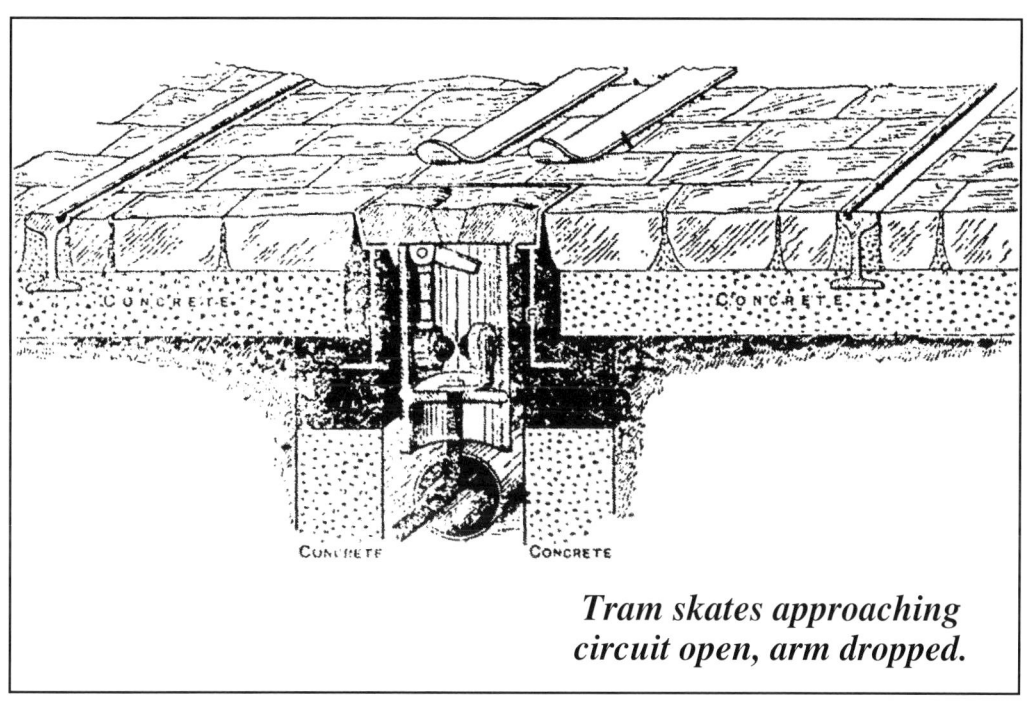

*Tram skates approaching circuit open, arm dropped.*

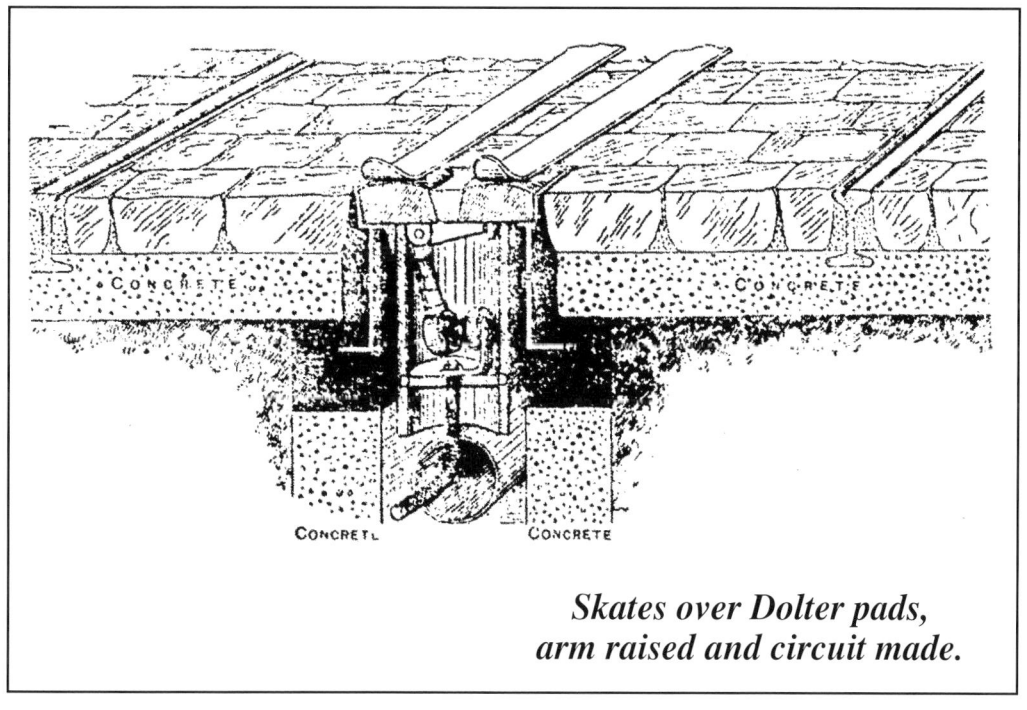

*Skates over Dolter pads, arm raised and circuit made.*

# CONVERSION TO OVERHEAD

The Tramway Company proposed that including the recently opened section from Vaughan Parade to the Grand Hotel be on the overhead current collection system. Torquay Council considered this the thin edge of the wedge for a total conversion from surface to overhead and the dispute went to arbitration. An inquiry into the Dolter system on the original lines commenced on 4th April1907 and it should be noted the Board of Trade was concerned at the number of problems being experienced with the Dolter system, and this may have influenced matters. The outcome was in favour of the tramway company and it was decided to convert the whole of the tramways to overhead current collection. Another pertinent matter was the cost of current which it was estimated cost 20% more for the Dolter system than overhead.

Finally the proposed new tramway to Paignton was agreed between the two councils and following withdrawal of the objection by the Great Western Railway the Bill was passed and appropriate powers were obtained which stipulated that the overhead system be used throughout from Vaughan Parade to Paignton. During the course of construction Paignton Council pressed for a much higher charge for current supplied within their boundary than in Torquay despite the fact they did not own the generating station although they had powers to buy it in the next few years. However operation to Paignton commenced on 17th July 1911 immediately following an inspection. The extension to Paignton had necessitated the purchase of twelve new trams (later increased to fifteen) and the construction of a new depot at Preston. Whilst this new tramway was under construction and as a result of Board of Trade authorisation conversion of the other tramways from surface to overhead current collection was undertaken costing £60,000 and using 448 poles and fifteen miles of copper wire. In general the structure was poles with bracket arms (with one centre pole in the Strand) but at certain places span wires were used at certain junctions and throughout the Paignton extension. Completed on 6th March the overhead was approved. An interesting innovation was the fitting of meters to the trams to show the consumption of current and a bonus was paid to drivers who were economical.

A combination of high tides and storm force winds can result in sea water and debris being spread across the seafront especially between the Grand Hotel and Belgrave Road .Permission was given to construct an avoiding route from the Grand Hotel to Castle Circus via Rathmore Road, Falkland Road, Lucius Street, and Tor Church Road was given but the tramway was not constructed. The final route length of the system was 9.19 miles (14.7km).

With the increased efficiency from the overhead system and extra business from the Paignton extension, the tramways prospered as shown below;-

| Year | Passengers | | Year | Passengers |
|------|------------|---|------|------------|
| 1908 | 2,580,420 | | 1911 | 3,594,317 |
| 1909 | 2,707,564 | | 1912 | 4,207,619 |
| 1910 | 2,876,573 | | 1913 | 4,832,684 |

Car miles    1910 - 382,809    1911 - 494,468    1912 - 626,478

The through fares of the services operated were Strand to Paignton 3d, Strand to St Marychurch via Ellacombe 2d and via Wellswood 3d. Beacon Quay to Torre station and Torre Station to St Marychurch were respectively 2d.

During the summer season special tourist trams were operated on the circular routes commencing at the Strand (clock Tower) and return at 1 shilling. Consequent upon the opening of the Babbacombe Cliff Railway in 1926 this ticket included a return ride on the Babbacome Cliff railway. A similar tour was operated from Paignton with passengers transferring from the Paignton service to the circular car at the Strand. Prior to World War one if passengers so desired the tram would stop at Babbacombe Downs Road for them to walk along the Downs escorted by the conductor. The driver would proceed to drive the tram slowly to the loop at St Anne's Road and await the return of passengers and conductor!

Insofar as the Torquay trams were concerned the years 1912-1918 were relatively uneventful and World War one did not seriously affect its operations although early, late and Sunday services were reduced and a large number of staff enlisted in the armed forces. Of the original forty two conductors all enlisted except three who were unfit with the result that boys were taken on as conductors. The company guaranteed their jobs back to those who volunteered and paid their wives seven shillings and sixpence (37.5p) per week and one shilling and six pence (12½p) for each child per week. The staff remaining behind set up a fund by which two old pence in the pound each week was deducted from their wages for the dependants of any who gave their lives or for those who returned disabled. Regrettably three of the brave young men who volunteered made the supreme sacrifice. In 1915 receipts were down to £14,338 and car miles 292,624 but in 1916 the position improved with revenue at £30,814 and car miles 471,373.

On Thursday 25th January 1917 a storm force gale and heavy rain blew the car working the 11.20 pm staff car from Paignton off the rails as it approached Kings Drive. Another car ran down from the depot and the derailed car was re railed and it was towed back to the depot. (Cars were equipped with a tow bar and pins).There was no service to and from Paignton on the Friday until late in the day but at 6.05 pm number 8 was blown off the track near Kings Drive. Regrettably the car caught fire and when extinguished the remains were taken back to Westhill Avenue depot and it was not until the Sunday afternoon that the service was resumed. After the war no. 8 received a new body and controls. The company was alive to the potential of motor transport for a rapid post war growth and in 1919 announced its proposal to initiate regular motor bus services on interurban routes embracing Newton Abbot, Teignmouth, Dawlish, Exeter, and Torquay. The first route commenced in May 1920 between Torre and Newton Abbot and was followed soon after by Newton Abbot-Dawlish. This new development brought the Tramway Company into direct and intense competition with the Devon General Omnibus and Touring Company Limited which had been formed at Exeter on 22 May 1919 with the intention of providing bus services in the immediate catchment area of Exeter and to link Exeter with Newton Abbot and Torquay and to commence bus services within the latter two places.

In June 1922 the conflict was resolved when the Tramway Company obtained a controlling interest in Devon General and reconstituted the Board of Directors and in 1931 the National Electric Construction Company Limited (of which Devon General was now a subsidiary) became part of the British Electric Traction Company. Two months later the tramway buses were transferred to Devon General giving a combined fleet of 42 buses and 13 char-a bancs. Bus services were completely revised to avoid competition with the trams and to combat competition from other bus operators. Devon General was thus established as the predominant bus operator in the area, a position it has held to the present day now part of the Stagecoach group as Stagecoach South West.

The Tramway Company's bus fleet was kept in a garage built in 1920/21 alongside the tram depot in Westhill Avenue, Torquay where on 3rd June 1921 soon after 1.00pm a barrel of petrol became ignited and exploded causing severe damage to the premises and destroying one bus and damaging several others besides much damage that was caused to adjacent properties. Luckily most employees were at lunch but motor man Cornhill who drove several trams to safety out of the depot was badly burned and never returned to work receiving a lump sum payment from the insurance company and motorman Bishop, depot clerk Argus, and P.C.Kelly were injured. The main depot and six houses for staff accommodation were not completed until 1925 and the houses were later numbered 42 to 52 (evens) in St Margaret's Avenue adjacent to Westhill Avenue. When the Westhill Avenue depot ceased to be used for trams it was expanded to house the growing fleet of buses but when a new bus depot was constructed in Torquay, the Westhill Avenue depot ceased to be used for buses and it was used by the council to house refuse collection vehicles. Now the site is occupied by a block of apartments named "Tramways" which has a short length of track with granite setts and a marble commemorative plaque near the front door recording the site's previous history.

The Paignton route closed on 14th January 1934 and the remainder on 31st January 1934,the Tramway Company being wound up on 13th March 1935.

# ROLLING STOCK

The depot had six roads with pits, workshops and offices and it was to this depot that the first trams numbered one to eighteen were delivered beginning with number seven. Brought to Torquay by rail and unloaded at Torre station in semi dismantled state insofar as the upper deck seats were stored in the saloons and on the platforms during transit. Transferred from rail trucks to drays drawn by a team of horses they were taken to the depot where the bodies were lowered onto the trucks and the remaining assembly work undertaken. Built by Brush these open top cars seated twenty-two inside and twenty-seven outside and were mounted on Mountain and Gibson 8 feet 6 inch wheelbase radial trucks. A slightly unusual feature was that a transverse seat installed in the end curves of the top deck but later on some cars the transverse were replaced with curved seats.

The bodies of the original eighteen trams had three windows each side with curtains (removed in 1922 when they had become worn and grubby), half turn stairs, longitudinal seating covered with red plush on the lower deck for 26 passengers. These bodies were mounted on Mountain and Gibson four wheel 8 ft 6inch wheelbase radial trucks with two 35 horse power motos,B18 controllers and mechanical slipper brakes. The extension to Paignton required extra trams and fifteen were purchased and numbered 19 to 33.Numbers 19 to 30 were delivered in 1911 and 31 to 33 followed in 1912.To the same general specification as the original trams ,but seating 28 outside ,the bodies were mounted on Brill 21E short wheelbase trucks. In 1929 1,7,and 16 were retrucked with similar trucks and in 1930 numbers 9,10,17 and 18 were also retrucked but on 7 ft 6in wheel base Brill 21E trucks. An unusual feature of Torquay trams was an oil lamp fitted to the top nearside of the saloon bulkhead .These was for use in the event of a power failure. During 1920s 11,14, and 15 received wire mesh guards around the top deck replacing the original ornamental grill work After the war route boards painted with black lettering on a white background and showing the route were displayed on the lower rail of the central lower deck window.

In 1921 three single deck trams were purchased second hand from the Taunton Electric Traction Company Limited consequent upon the closure of that company in the same year. Built by Brush in 1905 the bodies were mounted on Brush six foot wheelbase A1 trucks with two 20 horse power motors .Several alterations were made to these cars including the fitting of trolley retriever ropes and conversion to 22 seats for "one man pay as you enter" operation. They worked on the Torre station –St Marychurch route in winter and in the summer months were stored at Paignton depot and not used at all after 1932.

The final additions to the fleet were six open top cars with bodies built by Brush and mounted on Brush 3L maximum traction bogie trucks fitted with 40 horse power motors and Hoffman roller bearings which ensured they gave a very smooth ride. The first two delivered in 1924 were numbered 37-38 and 39 and 40 in 1925. These four cars which had five windows each side, and had vestibules were 36 feet 8 inches long and because of the track gauge 6 feet 6 inches wide. Longitudinal seating was provided inside and transverse seating outside giving a total seating capacity of 76 passengers. In 1928 two similar cars, numbered 41 and 42, entered service but seating was reduced to 72 because transverse seating was used inside These cars were fitted with plain bearings and half light windows which opened inwards instead of outwards as on the original four and they also had a wire mesh guard around the upper deck in place of the ornamental grillwork fitted to other Torquay trams. The controllers were fitted with dead man's handles on the controllers and the destination indicators were set lower on the guard rails. When the Torquay tramway closed these six bogie cars were sold to Plymouth where they operated until 1939.Original cars 7, 9, 10, 16, 17, and 18 were also sold to Plymouth where they operated for four years.

The livery of the trams was maroon on the waist panels, sole bar, dash and stairs, lined in gold and cream on the rocker panel and window surrounds, and the elaborately lined corner window pillar Numerals were carried on the dash in gold relieved with pink (some were blue) and the large lettering on the rocker panels was in gold, relieved with blue. The original lettering was THE TORQUAY ELECTRIC TRAMWAYS. This is unusual in carrying the word THE, and has not been general practice. Over the years trams did not necessarily receive a full repaint but went through a process known as "Touch up and varnish" (TUV).This had the effect over time of making the maroon appear brownish and the yellowish cream or even orange. To increase revenue advertising on the trams was introduced in July 1912.Advertisements were also displayed on the backs of seats.

46.    This view of the Strand, Torquay in 1904 is not superficially much different over one hundred years later. The trams have yet to appear, public transport being provided here by two "Chelmsford" steam buses of the Torquay and District Motor Omnibus Company.

47.    Great Western Railway bus stands outside their office in Vaughan parade whilst working their Paignton –Torquay service. Note that track for the tramway has not yet been laid .The office is just to the left of the shop front in the previous photograph.

48. Track laying is seen in the Strand with Torwood Street to the left and Victoria parade to the right. The Dolter boxes can clearly be seen. The excavations were bought to road level by the insertion of wooden setts.

49. In this photograph the power cable linking the covered Dolter pods can be seen and to the side piles of wooden setts await insertion.

50. No machinery or mechanical aids appear to assist the workmen laying track in Union Street.

51. The new trams were delivered by the GWR to Torre railway station and transported to the depot in St Marychurch for fitting out and uniting with their trucks. They were transported on horse drawn drays.

← 52. Car no. 18 in the Strand is being driven on test by company workmen. As delivered the fleet name was THE TORQUAY TRAMWAYS COMPANY LIMITED but in later years THE was omitted on some repainted cars.

53. Three trams are lined up on Beacon Quay for the opening ceremony in April 1907. Motorman Charles Pugh supervises the Mayor who drove the official car no. 18. In the event only two cars were needed and the number of persons watching the event was small.

54. Following the official opening of the tramway no. 18 returns from the Strand into Beacon Quay. On the left is a steam bus of the Torquay Road Car Company, soon to disappear.

55. Number 4 moves off to follow 18 for the official opening. We must presume that 13 returned to the depot "not required."

56.     A small, but important send off for number 6 as it officially opens the circular service on 11 November 1907. The transverse seat instead of the more usual circular seat at each end of the top deck can be clearly seen.

57.     No. 8 was seriously damaged on 26th January 1917 when it was blown off the track in a severe gale. It received a new body and electricals after the war. The smartly turned out conductor with his cash bag and bell punch well illustrates the uniform of staff in the heyday of the tramways.

58. This view depicts the main depot at St Marychurch.

59. The four road depot leading off Torquay in Preston was established when the Paignton extension was introduced on 17th July 1911.

60. Number 15 is in Vaughan Parade with the mayor at the controls prior to driving the car to the Grand Hotel for the official opening of the extension on 16th April 1908.

61. Later the same day 15 is depicted in ordinary service still with its flags.

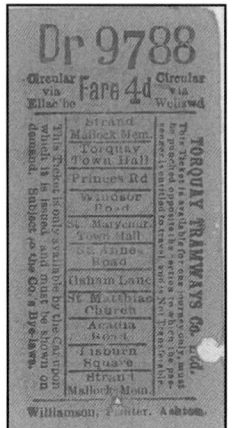

62. Track laying in Vaughan Parade is for the extension to the Grand Hotel. When the author was General Manager of Greenslades Tours Limited this was that Company's principal booking office in Torquay.

63. We observe the laying the wooden setts in Torbay Road adjacent to the Grand Hotel.

64. A car is depicted standing at Torre railway Station.

65. Number 14 is illustrated in the original livery further illustrating the transverse seats.

➔ 66. Trams working on the Dolter-system are seen snowed up in Fleet Street, Torquay on 27th January 1910.

67. In 1911 crowds at the carnival prevent the trams from moving.

68. Number 17 is near the Palm Court Hotel as it proceeds to Vaughan parade. It is quite clear that the Dolter system was installed here for double track.

69. Number 2 on route for Paignton has just left Preston.

70. Now working on the overhead, number 22 (of the second batch of cars) is on route to Paignton in 1911.

71. Belgian Soldiers are on an outing given by a Mr Oldfield in 1914 for wounded troops.

72. Further on from the Grand Hotel towards Paignton number 16 passes a horse drawn wagon outside Holicombe gas works in 1913.

73. New Zealand soldiers in Torquay parade with their Maori band.

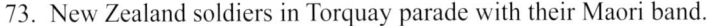

74. Travelling in the opposite direction to number 2 tram is number 37 which is rounding the same bend as it nears Preston.

75. A decorated tram in 1914 was used to raise funds for the wounded.

76. Here is one of the first batch of Torquay Tramway buses, number 9 (T8194).

77. Photo 46 shows buses soon to be replaced with trams, whereas in this photograph the tramway bus on the left is the beginning of the end for the trams, one of which has arrived from St Marychurch and is standing behind the Clock Tower.

78. A bogie tram proceeding towards Paignton has just passed the Palm Court Hotel which fronts the Abby Sands. This photograph shows how susceptible this area is to flooding arising from the combination of gales and high tides and is the area where number 8 was blown off the track in 1917.

79. In the Strand number 23 driven by motorman Frank Potter is passing an AEC "YC" an ex tramways bus absorbed into the Devon General fleet.

80. Torquay regatta in 1921 and number 23 is standing in front of the Clock Tower.

81. Number 6 is about to depart from the terminal stub track at Hyde Road Paignton to which 37 is approaching from Torquay.

82. This school special is being operated by number 9 (the driver of which is in plain clothes) which still carries the three lined out panels and the garter crest but the THE is no longer displayed in the fleet name. Was this the only one to be so treated because the new bogie cars were lettered The Torquay Tramways Company Ltd?

83. Bogie car 41 is seen at Paignton. This and all the other bogie cars were sold to Plymouth Corporation Tramways following the closure of the tramways in Torquay.

84. Standing at the end of the track at Beacon Quay, the trolley of number 1 has been swung but the controller handle has yet to be changed to the other end.

85. Viewing from the east end of the Strand, two cars on the circular service pass as no. 41 stands in Vaughan parade awaiting departure to Paignton.

86. This view shows the turning from Torquay Road into Hyde Road Paignton when nearing the end of this route.

87. No. 5 stands in Torwood Street about to commence a circular service in 1933.

88. Near the Palace Hotel (on the right) number 28 is seen on the spring operated passing loop.

89. In the Babbacombe area in 1925 numbers 25 and 4 pass near Odicombe Hall and St Albans Road.

90. No. 20, one of the second batch of cars, has just arrived at Ellacombe on a sunny day in 1929.

91.     St Marychurch Town Hall on the left of the photograph was the most northerly point of the system. The two trams in St Marychurch Road are proceeding in opposite directions.

92.     No. 34, one of the three single deckers purchased from Taunton tramways, has a rope attached to the trolley boom to retrieve the trolley in the event of a dewirement. Here the car passes over the points into Forest Road.

93. In 1926, number 11 one of the original fleet passes the Grand Hotel whilst on route to Torquay.

94. The location is The Royal Blue and other coach operators booking office in the former GWR office in Vaughan Parade. Number 11 has just arrived from Paignton.

95. No. 1 descends Forest Road on the service from St Marychurch to Torre railway station in 1927.

96. Heading for St Marychurch in 1933, Car 31 turns from Upton Road towards Lymington Road. The track arrangement was made necessary by the tightness of the corner.

97. At Torre station, no. 32 is destined for Beacon Quay and 33 to St Marychurch.

98. No. 15 arrives at the Paignton terminal in 1930.

99. On the same day no. 40 waits at the Paignton terminal prior to departing for Torquay.

100. Number 40 reverses at the Strand end of Vaughan Parade to return to Paignton. Note the conductor changing the trolley with a pole. As all the double deck cars were without ropes, it is presumed that at other terminals driver and conductor went on the top deck to grip the trolley to swing and rewire it.

101. Car no. 27 turns from Market Street into Union Street.

102. Car 32 descends the St Marychurch Road as it approaches the tram stop at Plainmoor and passes over the points leading the track into the main depot in Westhill Avenue.

103. Car number 28 is in the yard of the Westhill Avenue depot prior to taking up service.

104. Two of the single deck cars are pictured in the depot; the one at the rear is number 35.

105. This interior view shows St Marychurch depot in Westhill Avenue.

106. One of the first batch of Torquay trams mounted on a Mountain & Gibson truck has been photographed in Preston depot.

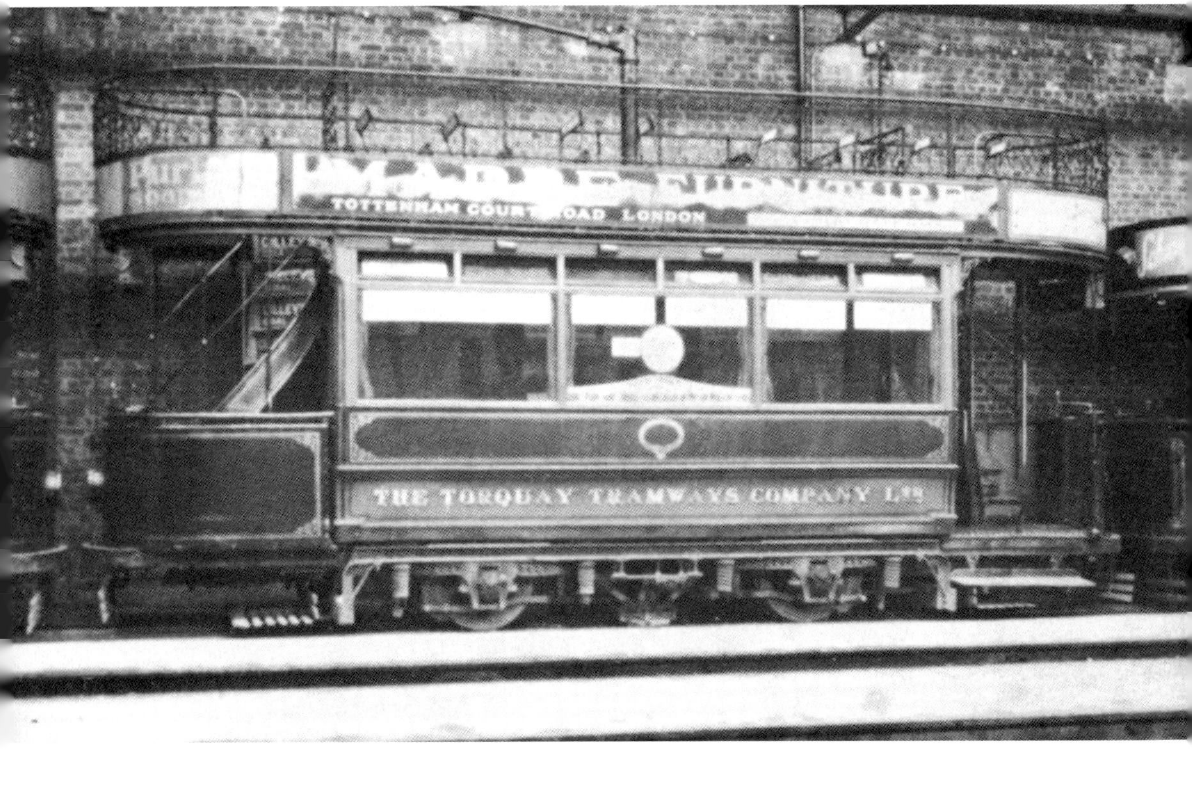

84

107. This view of ex Taunton single deck car was also taken in Preston depot. It carries the original livery.

108. This scene depicts the depot in Westhill Avenue after the explosion on 3rd June 1921.

109. The tramway staff are photographed outside the Westhill Avenue depot in 1911.

110. The final journey of a Torquay tram is about to commence on 31st January 1934 at the Strand, the tram proceeding via Fleet St, Union St., and Ellacombe to the depot at Westhill Avenue St Marychurch.

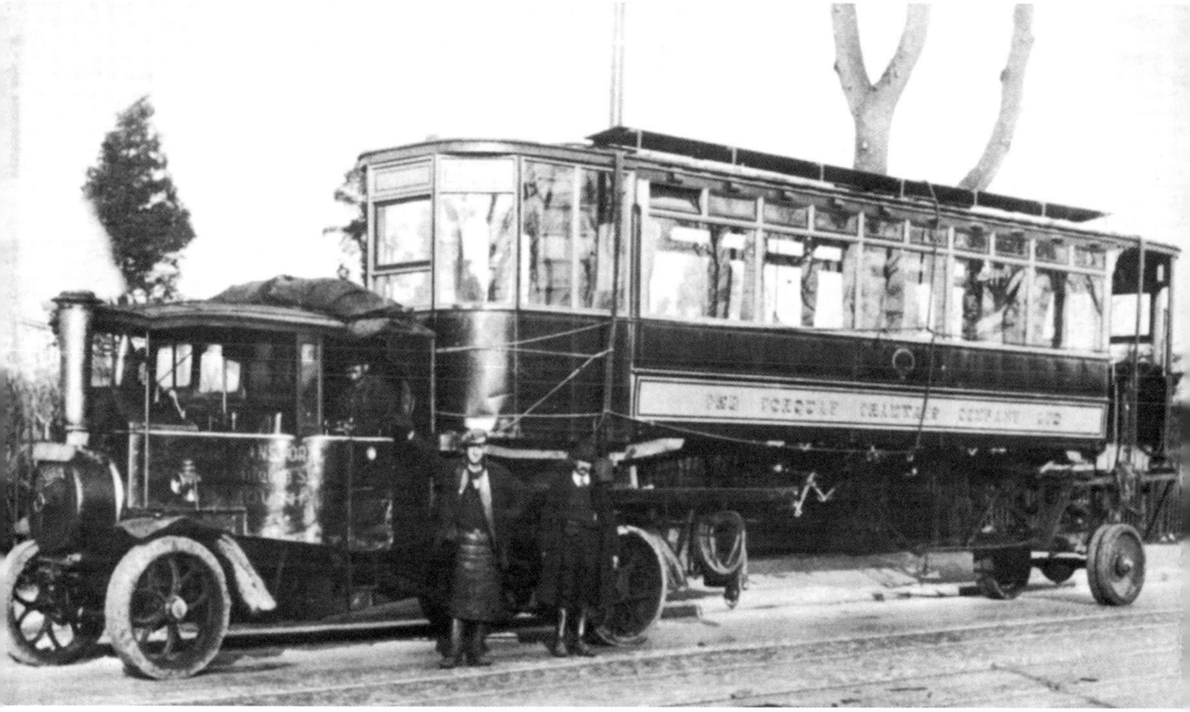

111. A Torquay bogie tram travels by road to Plymouth in 1933. It is hauled by a Foden steam wagon.

112. A rare view of a car (no 8) working on the Dolter system, as it proceeds along Manor Road in the leafy tranquilty of St Marychurch.

# 3. BABBACOMBE CLIFF RAILWAY

## HISTORICAL BACKGROUND

The Babbacombe area of Torquay is situated on the top of cliffs at the foot of which are the attractive Oddicombe beaches. Linking them was an obvious idea and in 1890 Sir George Newnes M.P. offered to build a cliff railway to connect the Downs to Oddicombe beach. As with most such projects there were supporters and objectors .A scheme put forward just prior to the outbreak of war in 1914 might have been successful had war not broken out in that year. It was not until 1923 that the Torquay Council promoted a Light Railway Order to construct a cliff railway. Following a public enquiry the Bill received Royal Assent and the Torquay Council leased the land to the Torquay Tramways Company. Their parent company the National Electric Construction Company under took the work of constructing the railway commencing on December 1924.The line is 720 feet (219.4 metres) long and transverse concrete foundations were laid at 21 foot intervals down the hillside. To these were fixed four reinforced beams each 17 inches deep and onto them transverse sleepers were laid. To these sleepers two parallel rails each weighing 105 lbs per yard were fixed by means of spikes to the standard gauge of 5 feet 10 inches (1778 mm) for two parallel tracks.

The line opened on 1st April 1926 and conveyed on average192, 000 persons per summer season, cars operating every few minutes. Fares at this time were 2d and 3d return. Perambulators, Push Carts, and luggage were charged for. When the Torquay Tramway Company ceased to function in 1934, the Babbacombe Cliff railway was purchased on 13th March 1935 by Torquay Corporation for £2,500 and continued to operate until 1941 when it was closed due to war time conditions and restrictions.

The two cars which were painted maroon and cream received bodies reminiscent of tramway pattern and were mounted on a four wheeled underframe with inside bearings. Longitudinal seating each side seated twenty passengers and there were doors at either end which opened directly onto corresponding doors at the top and bottom stations. The cars and operating equipment was constructed by Waygood Otis Limited. It operated on the counter balance principle which means that the weight of the descending car assists in lifting the other. The line is worked from a motor room situated below the upper station and the cable connecting the two cars passes around a drum which was driven by a 45 horse power DC variable speed motor through worm and pinion reduction gearing. This cable is formed of four wire ropes each 2½ inches diameter and as built had a breaking strain of 18 tons .A steel safety cable is also attached to each car so that in the event of the main one failing the tension on the safety cable would cause a spring loaded mechanism to operate, forcing steel teeth in the car under frame to lock into the track. The normal rate of descent is 500 feet per minute and should it rise to 600 feet per minute a governor automatically stops the motor.

After the Second World War, the line was not reopened until 29th June 1951 and much expensive reconstruction work was carried out. Prior to its reopening the cars were repainted in green and cream with the Torquay coat of arms on the side panels. The line soon regained its popularity and needed more capacity so in 1955 two new carriages able to convey forty standing passengers were built (and painted light blue with yellow around the windows and white roofs) by J and E.Hall Ltd of Dartford. This firm also supplied new machinery which increased the breaking strain of the safety cable to 21 tons. In 1993 the track was relaid and the lift reopened in 1995. For a period during the summer of 2002 during breakdowns of the railway, service was provided by two fourteen seat minibuses of Alansway of Newton Abbot using the narrow road between the beach and Babbacombe downs. The line has an excellent safety record and in 2003 the efficiency of the safety equipment was demonstrated when it activated as a result of a broken fish plate at the top of the east track and forcing the steel teeth into the track bed which stopped and lifted the car enabling the safe evacuation of the passengers. After being closed for six weeks the line was reopened.

Two further new cars to replace those supplied in 1955 were built and delivered in the late 1990s .Similar in appearance of the 1926 cars and finished in a livery of yellow lower panels with light blue window surrounds had five side windows with half lights but reverted to the livery of maroon and cream for the 80th anniversary in 2006. In 2005 the Friends of Babbacombe Cliff Railway was set up when there was a real threat that the railway would be closed. This group applied sufficient pressure for the Torbay Council to allocate the receipts from the sale of the St Marychurch Town Hall to the refurbishment of the railway during the winters of 2005/6/7 when restoration and renewal work was carried out. The railway, however, is still owned by Torbay Council but is operated under licence from them to the Babbacombe Cliff Railway Community Interest Company who has a forty year lease on the railway. Passenger numbers have varied over the years reaching 250,000 per annum but the total in 2010 was 86,000.

The basic fares for adults are £1.50 single and £1.80 return, children £1.00 and £1.20 respectively. Operating times are from morning to early evening daily from March until the end of October, weekends in November and December, and the February half term.

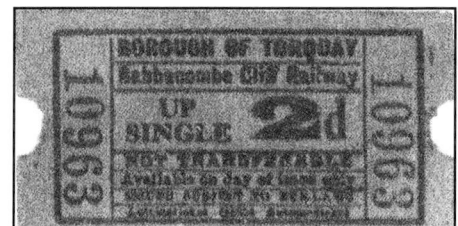
Borough of Torquay

Corporation of Torquay

1932 Survey.

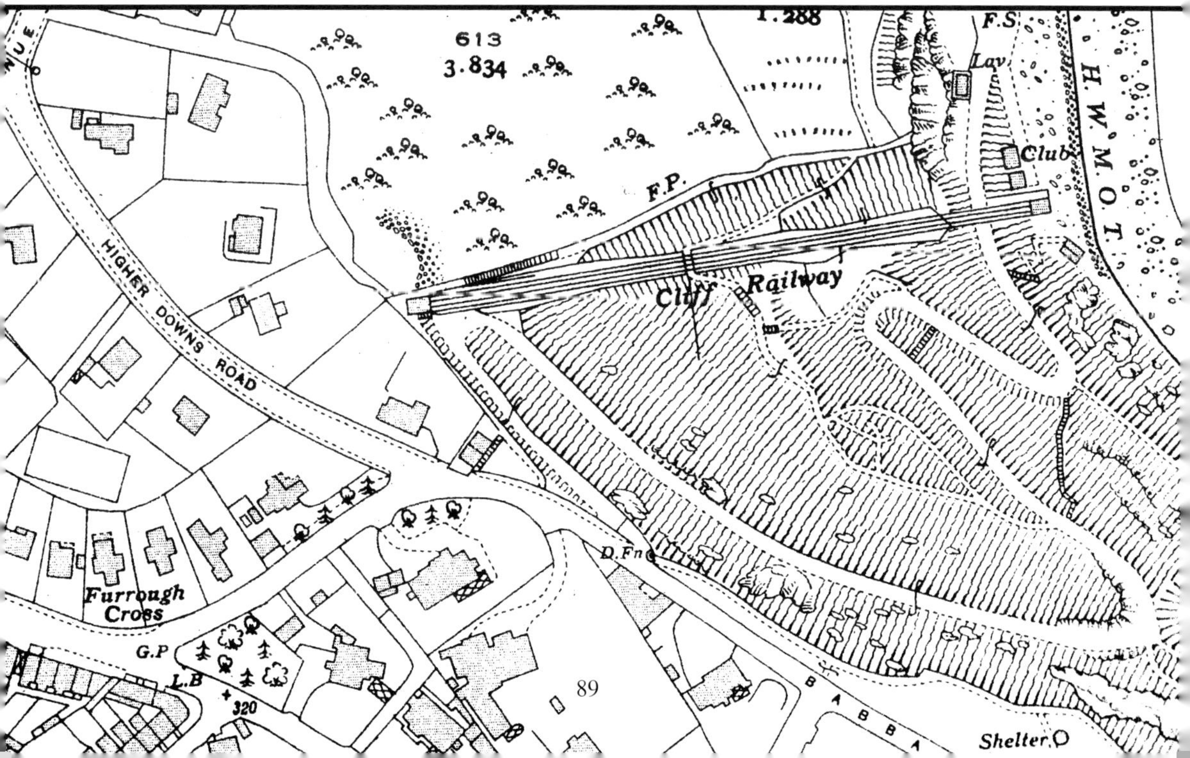

113. The opening of the Babbacombe Cliff railway took place on 1st April 1926. Note the construction of the truck chassis.

114. View from underneath a car at the Upper Station.

➔ 115. In this view seen upwards from the Lower Station, we can see how close the trees are to the track.

116. "Danger Low Bridge" In this photograph we can see a car at the lower station, adjacent to Oddicombe beach.

117. Two cars pass at the half way point.

118. The lower station at Oddicombe Beach.

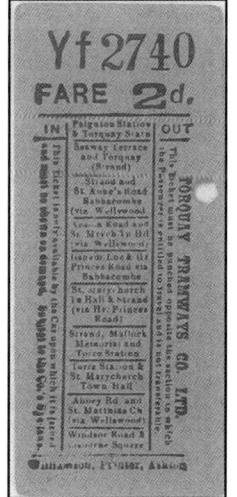
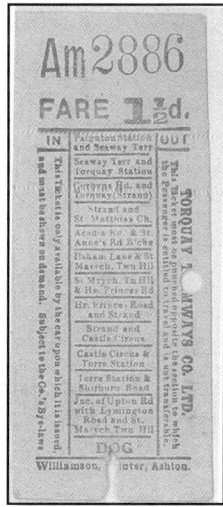

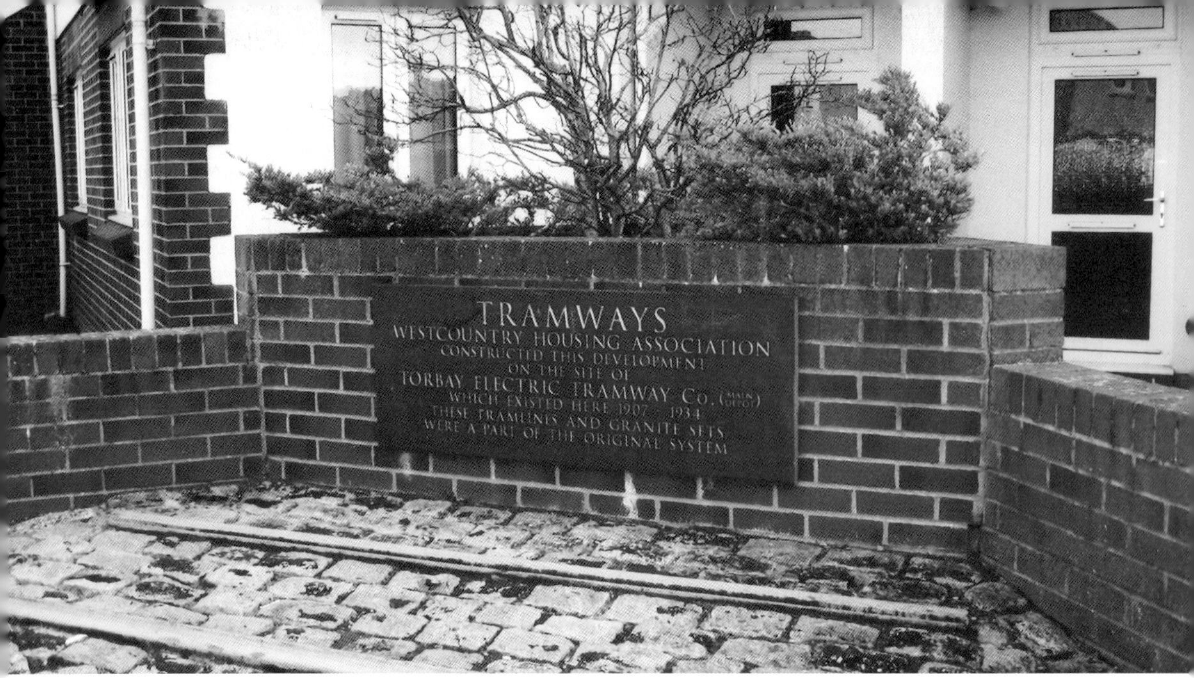

119.   Plaque and track set onto the wall surrounding the apartment block built on the site of the former tram depot in Westhill Avenue.

120.   We are at the upper station looking towards Babbacombe Downs. Showing one of the latest two cars.

121. Looking through the right hand door to the entrance of the car we catch sight of the interior of the upper station

122. This is the interior of the winding room.

# MP Middleton Press

**EVOLVING THE ULTIMATE RAIL ENCYCLOPEDIA**

Easebourne Lane, Midhurst, West Sussex
GU29 9AZ    Tel:01730 813169
email:info@middletonpress.co.uk

ISBN PREFIXES - A-978 0 906520  B- 978 1 873793  C- 978 1 901706  D-978 1 904474  E - 978 1 906008

\* BROCHURE AVAILABLE SHOWING RAILWAY ALBUMS AND NEW TITLES \*

**ORDER ONLINE** - *PLEASE VISIT OUR WEBSITE* - www.middletonpress.co.uk

## TRAMWAY CLASSICS  Editor Robert J Harley

| Title | Code |
|---|---|
| Aldgate & Stepney Tramways to Hackney and West India Docks | B 70 1 |
| Barnet & Finchley Tramways to Golders Green and Highgate | B 93 0 |
| Bath Tramways  Peter Davey and Paul Welland | B 86 2 |
| Blackpool Tramways 1933-66  75 years of Streamliners  Stephen Lockwood | E 34 5 |
| Bournemouth & Poole Tramways  Roy C Anderson | B 47 3 |
| Brightons Tramways  The Corporation's routes plus lines to Shoreham and to Rottingdean | B 02 2 |
| Bristol's Tramways  A massive system radiating to ten destinations  Peter Davey | B 57 2 |
| Burton & Ashby Tramways  An often rural light railway  Peter M White | C 51 2 |
| Camberwell & West Norwood Trys  including Herne Hill and Peckham Rye | B 22 0 |
| Chester Tramways  Barry M Marsden | E 04 8 |
| Chesterfield Tramways  a typical provincial system  Barry Marsden | D 37 1 |
| Clapham & Streatham Tramways  including Tooting and Earlsfield  J.Gent & J.Meredith | B 97 8 |
| Croydons Tramways  J.Gent & J.Meredith    including Crystal Palace, Mitcham and Sutton | B 42 8 |
| Derby Tramways  a comprehensive city system  Colin Barker | D 17 3 |
| Dover's Tramways to River and Maxton | B 24 4 |
| East Ham & West Ham Trys  from Stratford and Ilford down to the docks | B 52 7 |
| Edgware & Willesden Tramways  including Sudbury, Paddington & Acton | C 18 5 |
| Embankment & Waterloo Trys  including the fondly remembered Kingsway Subway | B 41 1 |
| Enfield and Wood Green Tramways  Dave Jones | C 03 1 |
| Exeter & Taunton Tramways  Two charming small systems  J B Perkin | B 32 9 |
| Fulwell - Home for Trams, Trolleys and Buses  Professor Bryan Woodriff | D 11 1 |
| Gosport & Horndean Tramways  Martin Petch | B 92 3 |
| Great Yarmouth Tramways  A seaside pleasure trip  Dave Mackley | D 13 5 |
| Hammersmith & Hounslow Trys  branches to Hanwell, Acton & Shepherds Bush | C 33 8 |
| Hampstead & Highgate Trys  from Tottenham Court Road and King's Cross  Dave Jones | B 53 4 |
| Hastings Tramways  A sea front and rural ride | B 18 3 |
| Holborn & Finsbury Trys  Angel-Balls Pond Road - Moorgate - Bloomsbury | B 79 4 |
| Huddersfield Tramways  the original municipal system  Stephen Lockwood | D 95 1 |
| Hull Tramways  Level crossings and bridges abound  Paul Morfitt & Malcolm Wells | D 60 9 |
| Ilford & Barking Tramways to Barkingside, Chadwell Heath and Beckton | B 61 9 |
| Ilkeston & Glossop Tramways  Barry M Marsden | D 40 1 |
| Ipswich Tramways  Colin Barker | E 55 0 |
| Keighley Tramways & Trolleybuses  Barry M Marsden | D 83 8 |
| Kingston & Wimbledon Trys  incl Hampton Court, Tooting & four routes from Kingston | B 56 5 |
| Liverpool Tramways - 1 Eastern Routes | C 04 8 |
| Liverpool Tramways - 2 Southern Routes | C 23 9 |
| Liverpool Tramways - 3 Northern Routes  A trilogy by Brian Martin | C 46 8 |
| Llandudno & Colwyn Bay Tramways  Stephen Lockwood | E 17 8 |
| Lowestoft Tramways  a seaside system  David Mackley | E 74 1 |
| Maidstone & Chatham Trys  from Barming to Loose and from Strood to Rainham | B 40 4 |
| Margate & Ramsgate Tramways  including Broadstairs | C 52 9 |
| North Kent Tramways  including Bexley, Erith, Dartford, Gravesend and Sheerness | B 44 2 |
| Norwich Tramways  A popular system comprising ten main routes  David Mackley | C 40 6 |
| Nottinghamshire & Derbyshire Try  including the Matlock Cable Tramway  Barry M Marsden | D 53 1 |
| Portsmouth Tramways  including Southsea  Martin Petch | B 72 5 |
| Plymouth and Torquay Trys  including Babbacombe Cliff Lift  Roy Anderson | E 97 |
| Reading Tramways  Three routes - a comprehensive coverage  Edgar Jordon | B 87 |
| Scarborough Tramway  including the Scarborough Cliff Lifts  Barry M Marsden | E 15 |
| Seaton & Eastbourne Tramways  Attractive miniature lines | B 76 |
| Shepherds Bush & Uxbridge Tramways  including Ealing  John C Gillham | C 28 |
| Southampton Tramways  Martin Petch | B 33 |
| Southend-on-Sea Tramways  including the Pier Electric Railway | B 28 |
| South London Tramways 1903-33  Wandsworth - Dartford | D 10 |
| South London Tramways 1933-52  The Thames to Croydon | D 89 |
| Southwark & Deptford Tramways  including the Old Kent Road | B 38 |
| Stamford Hill Tramways  including Stoke Newington and Liverpool Street | B 85 |
| Triumphant Tramways of England  Stephen Lockwood  **FULL COLOUR** | E 64 |
| Twickenham & Kingston Trys  extending to Richmond Bridge and Wimbledon | C 35 |
| Victoria & Lambeth Tramways to Nine Elms, Brixton and Kennington | B 49 |
| Waltham Cross & Edmonton Trys to Finsbury Park, Wood Green and Enfield | C 07 |
| Walthamstow & Leyton Trys  including Clapton, Chingford Hill and Woodford | B 65 |
| Wandsworth & Battersea Trys  from Hammersmith, Putney and Chelsea | B 63 |
| York Tramways & Trolleybuses  Barry M Marsden | D 82 |

## TROLLEYBUSES  (all limp covers)

| Title | Code |
|---|---|
| Birmingham Trolleybuses ... David Harvey | E 19 |
| Bournemouth Trolleybuses ... Malcolm N Pearce | C 10 |
| Bradford Trolleybuses ... Stephen Lockwood | D 19 |
| Brighton Trolleybuses ... Andrew Henbest | D 34 |
| Cardiff Trolleybuses ... Stephen Lockwood | D 64 |
| Chesterfield Trolleybuses ... Barry M Marsden | D 51 |
| Croydon Trolleybuses ... Terry Russell | B 73 |
| Darlington Trolleybuses ... Stephen Lockwood | D 33 |
| Derby Trolleybuses ... Colin Barker | C 72 |
| Doncaster Trolleybuses ... Colin Barker | E 92 |
| Grimsby & Cleethorpes Trolleybuses ... Colin Barker | D 86 |
| Hastings Trolleybuses ... Lyndon W Rowe | B 81 |
| Huddersfield Trolleybuses ... Stephen Lockwood | C 92 |
| Hull Trolleybuses ... Paul Morfitt and Malcolm Wells | D 24 |
| Ipswich Trolleybuses ... Colin Barker | D 59 |
| Maidstone Trolleybuses ... Robert J Harley | C 00 |
| Manchester & Ashton Trolleybuses ... Stephen Lockwood | E73 |
| Mexborough & Swinton Trolleybuses ... Colin Barker | E 36 |
| Newcastle Trolleybuses ... Stephen Lockwood | D 78 |
| Nottinghamshire & Derbyshire Trolleybuses ... Barry M Marsden | D 63 |
| Portsmouth Trolleybuses ... Barry Cox | C 73 |
| Reading Trolleybuses ... David Hall | C 05 |
| South Shields Trolleybuses ... Stephen Lockwood | E 11 |
| Tees-side Trolleybuses ... Stephen Lockwood | D 58 |
| Wolverhampton Trolleybuses 1961-67 ... Graham Sidwell | D 85 |
| Woolwich and Dartford Trolleybuses ... Robert J Harley | B 66 |